Contents

Preface

'Ideas for books come at funny moments' (Robert Westall). Our idea for this one came during a visit to Airedale Library and Family Centre in Castleford. Early years librarians are very good at telling other people's stories – this book is written to tell their story.

Producing this particular story – the book! – has not been a linear process. Our collaboration, between colleagues from two different disciplines has built on one another's diverse experiences to create the end product. Our partnership combines best practice in the two fields of early years education and information and library services. Drawing on each other's experience is one way that new ideas and better and more informed stories are told. The knowledge presented in the book is not all new, but has been refined and developed through listening to each other's decades of experience within our particular fields. What has been most exciting has been the way in which we think along the same lines, although we may take different routes to the goal. We hope the results are both informative and interesting, as we review policy and professional practice in early years services within library settings. We believe that the way this book has been collated and the professional practice it promotes are fairly new to the disciplines, and we hope that the way in which theory and practice has been blended is useful and innovative. This book would not have been written without practitioners, parents and families sharing their knowledge and providing rich examples. We have capitalized on their experiences – taking advantage of shared episodes from professional and family lives.

There's so much to discover in a good book!

We want to help early years librarians find a voice in promoting and sharing their own professional experiences and expertise - that is, how they develop and provide services that support young children and their families. This may often be achieved by working in partnership with others. Traditionally, library services for the child did not necessarily include parents and carers but early years library provision extends the traditional boundaries through being inclusive and reaching a range of audiences. Partnership programmes are important and libraries can help to build social capital by providing a safe place for people to meet, socialize and relax. We hope you will feel confident in using some of the ideas and activities from this book in your own setting. Be inspired and encouraged to put them into practice! If in doubt, tell a story.

Carolynn Rankin
Avril Brock

Introduction

This is a user-friendly professional book with a structure and format intended to make its content accessible to the reader. It is aimed at a professional market of practitioners working in early years librarianship. According to the Museums, Libraries and Archives Council (MLA), 'Museums, libraries and archives are uniquely placed to support families and early years children. They are based in the community and offer accessible learning opportunities that particularly support inter-generational groups' (MLA website). The generic message is that reading with young children is important and this book introduces the context in which early years language and literacy development occurs, looking at various UK government initiatives that underpin literacy. The book includes practical guidance on setting up library services for pre-school children and their parents and carers. The key role of the early years professional and the importance of effective interdisciplinary teamwork are examined, with a focus on involving parents and carers and valuing their culture, language, heritage and community. Library planning and design for pre-school children is covered, and practical advice to the librarian on how to negotiate with architects is provided. Collection development for both children and their parents and carers is considered, with practical guidance on selecting and using resources.

Case studies and scenarios are included throughout to tell the stories of a number of pre-school library initiatives, drawn from UK and inter-national sources. They provide examples of good practice and show that the key issues have an international dimension. Examples are provided from Wakefield Local Authority in West Yorkshire and Blackburn with Darwen Borough, where embedding libraries for young children and their families in Sure Start children's centres has been pioneered. These have proved to be extremely successful in promoting family involvement in early reading. We are aware of many other successful ventures, and although some early years librarians do publish details of their programmes and activities the information is not always easy to find. Other local authority programmes are presented, as are a range of national and international initiatives.

Sure Start, a government programme aimed at achieving better outcomes for children, parents and communities, began in the UK in 1999, working with a range of agencies in health, employment and education. Key elements of the programme are early education for all, increased quality and quantity of childcare, and working within local communities to develop local projects. The government's strategy is to develop 2500 Sure Start children's centres by 2008, with the longer-term aim of 3500 centres by 2010, one for every community (Sure Start website). The Effective Provision of Pre-School Education (EPPE) (DfES, 1999–2002) research demonstrates the importance of parents in children's early educational achievements. The Museums, Libraries and Archives Council (MLA) is working with the Department for Children, Schools and Families (DfCSF) and Sure Start to develop and strengthen the place of libraries in the government's programme for families and children. There is now a powerful base of more than 200 early years staff delivering Sure Start through libraries, and libraries are in the process of 're-creating themselves as family friendly environments' (MLA website).

The audience

The book is aimed at professionals with an interest in library and early years provision and is intended to provide a sound background in various aspects of pre-school library services. It is a practical guide for those who have to plan strategically or deliver early years library services and programmes at a local community level and a useful starting point for those who require the foundations of early years literacy. The DfCSF's new Early Years Foundation Stage (EYFS) became statutory in 2008 for children from birth to five years. Practitioners, including early years librarians, teachers, nursery nurses, play-group leaders and childminders require knowledge about how to deliver all aspects of the EYFS, meeting all young children's needs including promotion and encouragement of their communication, language and literacy skills. This book will provide knowledge and understanding about early language and literacy development and how young children become successful through enjoyable and meaningful experiences.

The book will be a valuable text for senior library practitioners with responsibility for the strategic planning of programmes and for children's librarians involved in delivering services at a local community level. It will also be of interest to managers of Sure Start children's centres and head teachers in schools, as well as to a range of early years practitioners working within the diverse early years services. It will be useful to those who work with children in local authorities, implementing the programmes for change through remodelling the integrated local children's services for the government's Children's Workforce Strategy. Its accessible text offers knowledge and ideas to increase confidence in working with other key professionals in delivering services and programmes. There are examples from best practice – what others have tried and what works well. The book enables early years librarians and practitioners, managers and local authority workers, communities and families to tell their stories. Although the book's key focus is UK-based, it should also be appropriate for librarians and early years professionals internationally, as it both draws on international practice and disseminates good practice developed in the UK. There is documented evidence of interest in developing these types of pre-school library and literacy activities in many other countries, including Australia, Canada and the USA.

This book will be a necessary read for postgraduate and undergraduate students on CILIP-accredited courses in the UK and students on library-related courses in other countries; library practitioners undertaking NVQ qualifications; and students on Childhood Studies courses who are planning to work in a range of services connected with children. We hope that it will encourage those embarking on a career in library work to consider early years settings.

Structure of the book

Each chapter has an introduction which outlines its content. All chapters include underpinning theory and contemporary research and are presented to inform professional practice. Knowledge and context present opportunities for discussion around key issues, and questions for practitioners. Case studies provide insights into experiences of early years practitioners in a variety of settings and illustrate examples of practice. Scenarios describe an event or series of actions so as to give insight into particular issues. They are included to demonstrate ideas and examples for practice. Activities and resources, checklists and 'how to' practical guidance, useful information on organizations, contacts and websites fill each chapter.

Acknowledgements

Thanks are due to all parents and children who provided information on their experiences for the case studies and scenarios in this book. We also have many practitioner colleagues to thank for their knowledge and contributions. Our original research project began with the early years library services provided by Wakefield Library and Information Services where Chris Barber, Cath Threapleton, Sue Wiggins and Carol Wootton introduced us to the Rainbow Library. Particular thanks are due to Carol Wootton who so willingly shared her practical knowledge and experience as a Sure Start librarian in Wakefield. Thanks are also due to Jean Gabbatt and Shelley Bullas from Darwen in Blackburn Library and Information Service for providing information on their successful partnership with children's centres in the authority. We are also grateful to Britta Heyworth and Lorraine Lee from Leeds Library and Information Services who told us about their early years projects. Thank you also to the students on the evaluation team for Earlystart, and to the staff, children and parents in the Bradford nurseries.

Thanks also to:

- Jackie Matthews for helping with the editing
- Flick and AJ for checking the early versions of the copy
- Staff in the British Library Boston Spa Reading Room
- Eddie Halpin for creating space and providing academic encouragement.

We hope you will like the photographs in the books and thanks are due to Alex, Brian, Isaac, Jack, Jessica, Kyran, Melissa, Rafferty, Richard, Shelley and Valerie. Thanks to Jane McGaughey for the photograph on page x and Chrystel Bijasson-Elliott for the photograph on page 51.

Finally, sincere thanks to our families for their support and patience during the writing of this book. We haven't dared tell them yet that we're planning another one!

Carolynn Rankin
Avril Brock

1

Take them to the library – setting the scene

Introduction

Literacy and communication skills are vital in society today and an early introduction to literacy through a breadth of experiences of rhymes, stories, pictures and books supports these skills. Encouraging young children and their families to access a library with all its resources can provide a great foundation for developing early literacy. There are many routes into reading and practitioners – early years librarians, carers and educators – should capitalize on all of them. Parents are in the best position to introduce their children to the world of words and families can be attracted into the library services by the range of practitioners who work with young children. Early years librarians need to provide positive conditions for all children and their families, so they can access the vast range of books and literacy resources available within libraries. Did you know that a major study of reading (Kirsch, 2002) concludes that reading for pleasure is more important to a child's educational achievement than its family's wealth or social class?

Children's services are receiving a high profile today, as policy-makers are concerned about effective education and the level of reading skills for the Information Age. This first chapter aims to set the scene for early years practitioners in terms of the UK government agenda. The political policies that influence and shape what is offered to our communities and how it will be delivered will be explored. It is important for practitioners to be effective in developing and delivering a range of services to meet local needs, using the techniques of community profiling. This chapter examines a range of issues related to meeting community needs. Proactive library authorities will use community profiling to develop and customize services to meet the needs of their local communities. Community profiling will be further explored in Chapter 2. Funding, sustainability and accountability are at the centre of most initiatives, but many practitioners may not be aware of the political landscape in which services are delivered. How strong is your professional voice in your parent organization or multi-agency setting? This chapter will explain how important your provision is within the increasingly complex landscape of early years provision in the UK. As an early years practitioner you are an advocate for literacy, and your practices are the tools of such advocacy. Providing resources, developing and delivering services, connecting with young children and their families all create communities of practice. This chapter provides examples of effective schemes between public libraries and other partners.

An overview of early childhood services

Over the past decade, many countries have developed their policies for early childhood education and care (ECEC). Early childhood is now high on the political agenda globally, shaping children's and their families' daily and future lives through policy development. This has evolved through the growing awareness of the significance of the first five years of life for intellectual, social and emotional development and the growing interest and research in these early years from the disciplines of psychology, education, social policy, social care and neuropsychology. This interest in policy has been stimulated by recent studies highlighting that the nurturing, care and education received from parents and carers are vital for optimal brain development, emotional intelligence, learning and educational achievement. There is growing evidence 'from neuroscience, from longitudinal development studies and from population studies that the period of early childhood is crucial in establishing a child's self identity, learning and achievement' (Gammage, 2006, 236). The past 20 years have seen exceptional developments in knowledge about how the brain develops, how genes and the environment interact to affect maturation (Shonkoff and Phillips, 2000). Policy development for early years services is therefore a complex process both conceptually and practically.

A key factor underlying policy development in ECEC is the view that a 'good start' in early education might be a way of compensating for any negative effects of children's developmental context (Sylva et al., 2004). The Effective Provision of Pre-School Education (EPPE) (DfES, 1999–2002) longitudinal research on ECEC, funded by the DfES, is a notable study in the field. The project aims were to identify the impact and effectiveness of pre-school on children's intellectual and social/behavioural development. It demonstrated the importance of parents in children's early educational achievements. Wilkie (2002) uses positive evidence from the EPPE project in her introduction to a Youth Libraries Group publication. 'When Professor Kathy Sylva, the principal investigator for the Effective Provision of Pre-School Education (EPPE) research team was asked by the Parliamentary Select Committee on Education and Employment "What is it that parents should do in those early years?", she replied "Take them to the library".'

Literacy is a human right

Basic education, within which literacy is the key learning tool, was recognized as a human right in 1948 in the Universal Declaration of Human Rights. In 1989 the United Nations endorsed the Convention on the Rights of the Child, which afforded children the same range of civil, political, economic, social and cultural rights as adults. It is the most complete statement of children's rights ever produced and it came into force in the UK in 1992. It requires that services for children develop policies that are responsive to the wide range of children's needs, encompassing all spheres of their lives (Lewis and Lindsay, 2000).

The Convention on the Rights of the Child is the first legal instrument to focus solely on the child, regardless of where the child was born and to whom, and regardless of sex, religion and social origin. It sets out in detail what every child needs to have for a safe, happy and fulfilled childhood. The rights focus on three key aspects – the three 'Ps' of protection, provision and participation. All of the rights in the convention apply to all children and young people without discrimination. These include the rights to:

- receive special protection measures and assistance
- have access to services such as education and health care
- develop their personalities, abilities and talents to the fullest potential
- grow up in an environment of happiness, love and understanding
- be informed about and participate in achieving their rights in an accessible and active manner.

Key rights include the right to education, the right to literacy and the right to play. Literacy is acknowledged as a major global issue and the UN has established the Literacy Decade from 2003 to 2012.

> Literacy takes many forms: on paper, on the computer screen, on TV, on posters and signs. Those who use literacy take it for granted – but those who cannot use it are excluded from much communication in today's world.   **UNESCO**

Libraries and librarians are a vital aid to literacy development, providing resources to help parents make sure their child has the best start in life. The generic message is that reading with young children is important, irrespective of first language, heritage or cultural background. The pleasure of stories and storytelling is universal and this will be explored further in Chapter 5.

A working group from the Chartered Institute of Library and Information Professionals (CILIP) provided an overview of library services to children and young people in the *Start with the Child* report published in 2002. This is at the centre of advocacy activity and argues that libraries can change children's lives. Books can inspire imagination, help emotional growth and develop understanding of the world and our place in the local and global community, past and present.

> Libraries are a hugely important part of children's and young people's lives because they bring books and children together; they provide reading opportunities free of charge, and so they encourage experimentation and learning.
> (CILIP, 2002, 9)

In many areas, the public library service works in partnership with early years services to provide multi-agency services that are flexible and meet the needs of young children and their families.

> The family support workers would tell everyone about the library and they'd bring them down to the library for a visit. They see it as their own, it's not just a library for Sure Start but for all the partners working with it.   Senior Librarian

The role of the public library in supporting young children

The International Federation of Library Associations (IFLA) has produced guidelines for children's library services to help public libraries implement high-quality children's services. Published by the Libraries for Children and Young Adults Section in 2003, the guidelines state that:

> Library services have never been as important for children and their families all over the world as they are today. Access to the knowledge and the multi-cultural riches of the world, as well as lifelong learning and literacy skills have become the priority of our society. A quality children's library equips children with lifelong learning and literacy skills, enabling them to participate and contribute to the community.

IFLA also says that by providing a wide range of materials and activities, public libraries provide an opportunity for children to experience the enjoyment of reading and the excitement of discovering knowledge and works of the imagination. Children and their parents should be taught how to make the best use of a library and how to develop skills in the use of printed and electronic media (IFLA, 2003).

Since the late 19th century public libraries in the UK have been at the heart of their local communities, providing services for children and young people, reflecting the diversity of the population they serve. In the past public library services mainly focused on children who already knew how to read. Public libraries are now actively encouraging parents and carers of babies and very young children to join in language and literacy activities.

The UK's Labour government views the way out of poverty to be through education and a high level of literacy and has committed funding to targeting 'effective' early childhood education and care (this will be explored in a later section in this chapter). Sustainability is dependent on links with other mainstream activities and funding opportunities and libraries also are involved in this particular focus on those at risk of social exclusion. Some individuals, groups or communities may feel deliberately excluded from access to mainstream services and may face barriers to using those services. This may be because of their own literacy skills, because they have never used libraries in their schooling years or because they have not found schools or other institutions to provide positive experiences. It is therefore important that early years services – children's centres, nurseries and libraries – welcome families and aim to meet all their clients' needs.

Public libraries have always been community spaces designed to support learning, reading and wider community objectives. Long-term benefits of early years services for the public libraries themselves can include improved understanding of target groups, a higher profile in the community and improved staff skills (Stevens, 2003). The public library service in the UK has many unique selling points and benefits. There is a strongly held view that libraries offer a welcoming, neutral space providing opportunities for personal, cultural and community development. Goulding (2006) writes about how public libraries are playing a role in multi-agency working and in enabling community involvement, cohesion and capacity building (2006, 237). Public libraries also give children and their families access to a vast amount of reading at all levels and for all interests. Ross et al. sum this up when they highlight the public library offer:

> The opportunity to try out a book with no risks and the importance of no-cost use, the assistance of knowledgeable staff, wide choice, and the ability to browse freely, choosing reading material independently, support readers of all ages.
> (Ross, 2006, 99)

Miranda McKearney of The Reading Agency believes that using the public library is an important first step in local citizenship. Children, and their families, can gain a sense of belonging to the community through using a shared resource and they are made welcome in a community space that celebrates diversity. This following case study will show the challenges librarians may face in providing support for family literacy in the communities they serve.

Case study

A librarian's reflection on the community her library serves

It's hard to get families into the library. We have plenty of school-age children, but we'd really like to get the younger children to come in too. I'm making that a priority. I've now started to visit and read stories in the Children's Centre next door. I found that most of the children are being brought to the Children's Centre by carers, but few parents seem to go there. It's very hard to make the connections. One grandma did not know her children's surnames and was not sure which father they had. It can be very difficult to get some parents to join libraries. We've found some would not enrol. They didn't want to fill in forms and we couldn't get them to bring their ID in. They had difficulties in filling in forms, as some had real problems with levels of literacy and couldn't fill in their address and postcode. Parents did not want the responsibility of having books in their homes. They wouldn't let the children borrow the books, as they thought they would have to pay fines. We try to be as welcoming as we can to draw these children and their families in through the doors.

Claire, community librarian

Evidence has shown that libraries are good at reaching hard-to-reach groups and can successfully build partnerships based on reading. For young children and their families there is the chance to develop and achieve in a community setting through accessing the local library. The Summer Reading Challenge is the largest UK reading promotion for young people aged 4–11 and it is organized by The Reading Agency. It is run in public libraries during the summer months and each year it takes a different theme. It challenges children to read at least six books during the summer holidays, which they keep track of in a special folder. There are incentives through stickers and rewards and children really enjoy the challenge, but it does help if their parents/families are involved in the scheme.

To support professional practice, practitioners should be aware of the political environment influencing the public library service and its partner organizations. *Framework for the Future* (2003) is the first-ever national public library strategy, setting out a long-term strategic vision that public libraries in England could aspire to by 2013. This suggests that public libraries should concentrate on three main themes: supporting early learning; supporting pupils and students; and supporting older students. Public library activities that promote reading are playing a key role in supporting learning. The Museums, Libraries and Archives Council (MLA) developed an action plan, funded by the Department of Culture, Museums and Sport (DCMS), outlining a range of projects and developments based upon the three main themes. *Books, Reading and Learning* is one of the four work strands of *Framework for the Future*. This outlines a series of projects and improvements to further the cause of reading in libraries and to support people of all ages in their reading development.

The role of early years librarians

According to IFLA, effective and professionally run children's libraries require trained and committed staff. Desired skills include:

- enthusiasm
- strong communication, interpersonal, team-working and problem-solving skills
- the ability to network and co-operate
- the ability to initiate, be flexible and be open to change
- the ability to analyse user needs, plan, manage and evaluate services and programmes
- eagerness to learn new skills and develop professionally.

The public library should be attractive to the early years community, as it provides access to library staff who know about children's books and care about children's reading. However, they not only need to be welcoming places, they also should be able to stimulate and inspire. Creative spaces should enable creative experiences and public libraries should provide a mix of cultural and creative resources and experiences. Many public libraries have strong links with writers, illustrators and storytellers and library practitioners get involved in holding events which draw in the local community. So, whether working in a large central library with extensive 'creative space' for running such events, or in a more modest local setting, practitioners can use the power of a storytelling, story-sharing experience to encourage and foster early literacy. The role of the early years librarian is therefore very important in drawing families into the world of literacy and all that it can offer.

Story time for pre-school children involves social learning, being part of the group, learning how to listen and following the activities modelled by the early years librarian. Creaser and Maynard (2006) note that throughout the UK 88% of public library services to children offer weekday sessions for 0–3 year olds and 85% for 3–5 year olds. These story and rhyme sessions for children are designed to help language development and reading skills. These activities now form part of the forward planning for library managers, and we look at more aspects of planning in Chapter 6.

Early years librarians not only have knowledge about stories, books and collection development (as illustrated in Figure 1.1 on the next page), but also about key initiatives and how to work in partnership with other organizations. For example, the National Literacy Trust (NLT) is an independent charity that changes lives through literacy and promotes reading to young families (NLT, 2002). The NLT links home, school and the wider community to inspire learners and create opportunities for everyone. The Talk to Your Baby initiative encourages parents and carers to talk to and enjoy communicating with their baby. There is a wealth of information about the initiatives of the National Literacy Trust and many varied, valuable resources available on its website. See the end of this chapter for details of this and other useful organizations.

Figure 1.1 An early years librarian preparing for a storytelling session

Bookstart

Early years librarians need to know about Bookstart, run by national charity Book Trust. It is the first national baby book-giving programme in the world. Bookstart began in the UK in 1992 with 300 babies; by 2001 there were over one million Bookstart babies. The scheme was initiated in 1992 by Book Trust, working in co-operation with Birmingham Library Services, South Birmingham Health Authority and Birmingham University School of Education (Wade and Moore, 1998). Bookstart operates through locally based organizations by giving a free pack of books to babies, with guidance material for parents and carers. The aim is that every child in the UK should enjoy and benefit from books from as early an age as possible. Bookstart for babies aged 0–12 months aims to provide a canvas bag to every new baby born in the UK, containing baby books, a booklet for parents setting out information and advice on sharing stories with young children, a Sure Start children's centres leaflet and a booklist and invitation to join the local library. The books are selected by a team which includes a health visitor and an independent expert on children's books. Choosing them is not as easy as it might sound: the varied cultural and social backgrounds of the children must be taken into account. In the majority of cases the Bookstart bag is given to parents by their health visitor at the eight-months health check. McElwee (2004) writes that Bookstart has been the catalyst for the development of new public library services aimed at this user group – such as rhyme times, interactive sessions using songs and action rhymes which encourage interaction between parent and baby – and to develop communication, bonding and enjoyment.

Children's rights

Library practitioners are at the forefront of promoting children's rights and helping to give young users the best start in life. They can play a key role in disseminating information about the importance of early literacy to parents, childcare providers, early childhood educators, children's advocates and political decision makers. Reflect on the following scenario.

Scenario: Having a voice as an advocate for early years policy

'Hello, what do you do?'

'I work as an early year's librarian in a children's centre'
'Gosh it must be great fun to spend all day just reading stories and running playtimes, though I'm not sure I could cope with all those little children crawling about . . .'

Reply option 1
'Yes, I do spend part of my day reading to young children and their parents and carers and helping them to choose books. It is great fun.'

Reply option 2
'Yes, I do spend part of my day helping young children and their parents and carers with story times and reading activities. I and my colleagues also address some of the key issues in 21st-century society – we tackle social exclusion, support lifelong learning. We encourage community cohesion and build social capital and foster cultural activity.'

Making parents and others in communities aware that librarians are a resource for early literacy information and guidance will help position libraries as community partners in the common public goal of helping children to become successful readers and learners. Libraries can change children's lives.

There is anecdotal evidence of the contribution libraries make to community agendas. To provide hard data, the DCMS and Museums Libraries and Archives Council (MLA) working with the Audit Commission and the libraries sector developed a set of public library impact measures which were launched in March 2005. The impact measures are a qualitative measure of performance, encouraging library services to assess their community profile and tailor services accordingly. They are also an advocacy tool aimed at decision makers outside library services. They demonstrate libraries' contribution to formal education, regeneration and community building. This inevitably impacts on the role of the early years librarian. The government's agenda is built upon targets and performance indicators. Public libraries, just like schools and other institutions, now have to demonstrate their value in supporting early learning and family learning through partnerships, for example, with Sure Start children's centres. The management aspects of service evaluation are discussed in more detail in Chapter 6.

There has been a significant increase in activity around early years provision in recent years and there are now many cross-sector initiatives, recognizing the key role of language in children's development. Multi-agency working and integrated service delivery are key aspects of government strategy to improve standards in the early years. Agency partnerships are helping parents to support their children's early language and literacy, as well as communicating important messages about emotional and social development and health issues. The challenge for librarians is to implement policies in libraries and work effectively with partners to achieve the effective delivery of services.

Policy and partnerships: Sure Start children's centres

The first five years of the New Labour government saw unparalleled attention, resources and initiatives devoted to early-childhood care and education as it 'rocketed onto the political, educational and research agenda' due to the commitment to reduce poverty and social exclusion (Taggert, 2004, 619). It targeted educational achievement to avoid the consequences of educational failure, juvenile crime, unemployment and teenage pregnancy, as highlighted in the USA Headstart longitudinal research findings (Sylva, 1994). Government investment in high-quality early-childhood education and care was to support educational achievement and potential and life chances, ameliorating the effects of social disadvantage.

The Single Regeneration Budget (SRB) programme was a seven-year government-funded initiative (DfES, 2000) aimed at areas of high unemployment, low income, and high numbers of bilingual/multi-lingual families. New initiatives were introduced in these disadvantaged neighbour-hoods, such as the Sure Start (DfEE, 1999) community-based local programmes aimed at supporting children, families and communities. Sure Start aimed to achieve better outcomes for children, parents and communities by increasing the availability of childcare for all children, improving health and emotional development for young children and supporting parents. Sure Start works in partnership with local authorities, Primary Care Trusts, Jobcentre Plus, local communities, public agencies and voluntary and private-sector organizations. These local programmes formed a central part of the government's anti-poverty agenda, seeking to integrate and expand health, childcare, early education and family-support services to families with young children living in economically deprived areas. The Sure Start mandate was to promote the physical, intellectual and social development of pre-school children so that they would succeed when they got to school. This included a focus on early language and reading.

The Children Act (2004) raised the degree of accountability, especially at local authority level. *Every Child Matters: Change for Children* sets out the national framework for local change programmes to build a fully integrated and holistic approach to services around the needs of children and young people, and takes forward the government's plans for radical reform for children, young people and families. This is a major new approach to the well-being of children from birth to age 19 and the aim is for every child, whatever its background or circumstances, to have the support it needs to:

- be healthy
- stay safe
- enjoy and achieve
- make a positive contribution
- achieve economic well-being.

The Sure Start (DfEE, 1999) community-based local programmes were integrated into the Sure Start children's centres and intended to be key in achieving the objectives set out in the *Every Child Matters* programme. In the 2006 ten-year strategy, the government promised to deliver a Sure Start children's centre for every community by 2010. Children's centres offer children under five years old and their families access to help from multi-disciplinary teams of professionals. The core offer of the centres includes integrated early learning, care, family support, health services, outreach services to children and families not attending the centre, and access to training and employment advice. Local authorities have a strategic responsibility for the delivery of children's centres. The programmes vary from area to area, as they are tailored to the needs of their particular community. The policies and programmes of Sure Start apply in England only; responsibility for early education and childcare in Scotland, Wales and Northern Ireland rests with the separate devolved administrations.

In a scoping study on family learning and public libraries in the UK, Spacey (2005) found that

> Libraries working with Sure Start would seem to be particularly successful in identifying and targeting new groups of families to involve in library activity. Indeed this would seem to be a reciprocal relationship, which benefits both libraries and Sure Start programmes. The employment of Sure Start librarians has been a significant development in the growing relationship between the early years and the library sector since Sure Start Local Programmes were first set up in 1999.   (Spacey, 2005, 32)

The results of the project in the study area indicate the importance of key professionals being willing to develop an interdisciplinary approach to achieve objectives. Early years librarians have been involved with the delivery of Sure Start programmes. During June 2006, and as part of their Families Love Libraries campaign, all 3500 public libraries promoted National Sure Start Month by organizing activities, creating displays and signposting local families to Sure Start events.

The government has contracted with a partnership of private-sector and public-sector organizations, called Together for Children, to provide delivery support on the ground for local authorities. The Together for Children website provides local authority resources, examples of good practice, case studies and discussion forums. This is a really complex area of provision involving many partnerships. Sure Start offers public libraries the opportunity to use partnership projects to target some of the hardest-to-reach families in a community. Libraries are key partners alongside children's centres in encouraging family reading. In some areas libraries and children's centres have formed very effective partnerships and are increasingly providing collaborative activities such as:

- coffee morning sessions
- storytelling events
- toy libraries
- reading sessions
- family literacy activities
- craft activities
- puppet shows
- information about childhood services
- information and resources about parenting.

The early years library: creating the right environment

Libraries should be safe and secure, as well as a welcoming environment for children. Long gone are the days of our expecting children to creep into a library, choose a book and creep out again. It is important to make information available to parents that will encourage them to bring their child to the library. The library should be a community hub - welcoming all. It is important to think about how the traditional barriers to access and use can be broken down and removed. In Chapter 3 we will look at some of the ways in which space and design can be used effectively to create a welcoming environment.

Young children will make the most of all their experiences in the library. They will enjoy the range of interesting materials to play with and the opportunity to socialize in a relaxed atmosphere. They will like the colourful environment and revel in the variety of sights, sounds and activities. If their parents and carers are relaxed and made to feel welcome this will enhance the experience for all and should lead to repeat visits. Word of mouth is an important means of promoting early years services. Important factors include very practical things such as ease of access to the building:

- If you are in a shared facility make sure the library is well signed to help potential users know where you are.
- Is there somewhere to park buggies and prams and leave car seats?
- Is it easy to get to the toilet and baby changing facilities?

(More of this in Chapter 3, when we will look at issues of space, design and planning.)

Positive outcomes from the Sunshine Library

Jane is a mum who, despite having literacy problems, is determined that her children will have better chances than she has had. She was encouraged to come to the library after receiving her Bookstart Plus Bag and listening to the Bookstart Plus worker on how to share books together.

A mum who has a daughter with Down's syndrome recorded the comment: 'I love to come to the Sunshine because nobody minds if you stay all afternoon.'

A mum who has mental health problems comes to the library for time out – she knows that our staff will make her feel welcome, make her a drink and read with her children – giving her some precious time for herself.

What practitioners need to know about young children

Some of you reading this book may already have a background in theories of early child development and pre-school literacy. However, many managers or co-workers may not have this knowledge base. In common with parents and carers, they will also have questions you may need to answer. The following sections highlight some of the underpinning knowledge and useful things to know about early literacy. This will help you to develop your role as an effective advocate for early years library services.

There are now many studies on the development of the brain that suggest that a young child's early years are important, as the learning that takes place during this time contributes to brain development and functioning. We learn as we interact with the world and the resulting stimulation of neurons in body and brain passes messages through the nervous system. This networking of the neurons effectively produces thought – the source of language. From thought comes meaning, and it is meaning that helps us to understand and interpret the world – the ultimate goal of any learning experience. Each new experience adds to the previous, to create a rich tapestry of learning and communication. The early interactions that occur between children and their parents and carers are crucially important for young children's personal, social, cultural, emotional and linguistic development. They not only promote close relationships and early language development, but also contribute to children's intellectual development. It is important for young children to have natural experiences and types of active learning, including 'brain gym', that will encourage thinking, learning and communication. Practitioners should be providing young children with the following opportunities to:

- have interaction with adults as listeners
- practise movements, sounds and rhythms
- practise language patterns repeatedly
- have opportunities for imaginative play
- discover and investigate creative means of expressing themselves
- be able to move around on their tummies to explore their personal space and the physical environment around them.

Children's centres, nurseries and libraries often provide rhyme, song, music and movement activities for young children. They will have interesting names such as 'Jo Jingles', 'Moving Minnies' and 'Sing-a-long with Sheree'. Baby yoga and baby massage are also on offer in many settings. These experiences are an important part of early literacy development, as well as being social activities with other children and their parents.

Librarians have always been interested in a 'reading child', but now, due to new understandings about child development and emergent literacy, we also need to be aware of the needs of babies and toddlers and provide opportunities to support their learning.

The Early Years Foundation Stage (EYFS)

Everyone who works with children from birth to five will need to know about the requirements of the Early Years Foundation Stage (EYFS), which is statutory from September 2008. The EYFS is a comprehensive framework for high-quality development, learning and care for all children from birth to the end of the academic year in which a child has her/his fifth birthday. The framework builds on and replaces the non-statutory Birth to Three Matters guidance, the Foundation Stage Curriculum Guidance for 3–4 year olds and the National Standards for Daycare (DfCSF, 2007). Each child and family is seen as unique, with differing needs and concerns. These are identified in the four key themes: A Unique Child; Empowering Relationships; Enabling Environments; Holistic Learning and Developments. The themes are linked to key principles, each of which has four commitments. Children's development is presented through six phases. These overlap and acknowledge that there can be big differences between the development of children of similar ages (DCSF, 2007). The EYFS stresses the importance of providing opportunities for children to communicate thoughts, ideas and feelings, and build up relationships with practitioners and each other. It also affirms the importance of promoting positive relationships with parents and families. Language and communication are key to learning and understanding.

Early years language and literacy development

Children need a multitude of experiences of oral language, of talking, listening, storying, rhyming, reading and singing. These are the building blocks of literacy and make the difference as to how quickly and easily they acquire reading and writing. Language is the key to learning, and promoting young children's language development can be an exciting journey (Brock and Rankin, 2008). Young children acquire language through interaction with others in their immediate environment, through responding to sounds, sentences and experiences expressed by their parents, family and other carers. They begin by absorbing, listening and then imitating and practising. Gradually they learn to reproduce sounds and words and establish an understanding of how language works, the structure and grammatical sense of putting these sounds and words together. When communicating and talking to their babies and young children, parents will accommodate their language use to promote attentive listening, understanding and then reproduction of sounds, words, then sentences.

Reading to babies and young children and getting them involved in that process is one of the most effective ways of enhancing language development in a child. Librarians have a number of great selling points - there is access to free books at the local library and children's centres and it is never too early for parents and carers to bring their babies and toddlers to the library. Encouraging the development of early language skills in children also means providing support and guidance for parents and carers. Babies can learn to handle books from a very young age. They will acquire vocabulary as parents and carers provide the words that match the pictures, imitating sounds with enthusiasm. The following case study illustrates the importance of involving babies in choosing books to read.

Case study

Amy, aged 8 months, and her books

Reading a book together now forms part of our daily routine. There is a large box full of books and before bed every night we choose a book to read together with the baby. Sticking a hand in the box and rummaging around makes an interesting noise and Amy responds excitedly. We do not specifically choose books for babies or young children, rather we read lots of stories together and she appreciates the rhythm and sounds made. Amy also likes turning the pages and will sometimes want to turn back to the first page. She is also excited by pages with particular colours on them.

Amy's mum tells us something about how they share the reading experience. Practitioners can advise parents that it is important to get into a routine with their baby. Each night before bed, it is good to choose a book together; it can be a very simple book with just a few words on a page. In holding a conversation with the baby, the adult provides an opportunity to model turn taking by waiting for the baby's response before continuing. The baby is also learning book-handling skills, even at this young age. This illustrates the importance of reading to babies and involving them in the process of choosing books to read. Although the baby may not yet be able to understand the words or articulate formulated responses, clearly she is enjoying the experience. She is looking at the pictures and learning how to turn the pages. Many books are quite tactile with different materials to touch and feel, flaps to lift up or buttons to press. It is good to point out that reading before bed can settle the baby and ensure that there are fewer interruptions during the night.

(Brock and Rankin, 2008, 27)

Emerging literacy

As you can see, young children don't wait to begin their early experiences of reading and writing until they start school! Children will acquire language and literacy skills from their earliest years. From birth and throughout pre-school years babies and young children develop knowledge of language and the sounds that form words. This places the onset of literacy acquisition at birth rather than at the start of formal reading instruction at school. Emergent literacy (Clay, 1991) is a term used for young children's early explorations into reading and writing. As they are singing rhymes, listening to stories, looking at pictures, handling books, scribbling and drawing with varied writing implements, they are acquiring early literacy skills.

Young children soon begin to incorporate patterns and incidents from stories into their everyday conversation. Stories can have a tremendous impact on many aspects of children's lives, permeating their language experiences and enabling them to use advanced linguistic structures (Fox, 1993). The following examples demonstrate how young children incorporate stories in their everyday activities.

Scenario: Early story experiences

Two-year-old Jeremy wore a pyjama collar round his neck for weeks because 'if you don't wear a collar, you get taken to the pound'. This originated from his first video of Walt Disney's *Lady and the Tramp* and it engendered lots of family storytelling. This two-year-old was able to use and understood 'pound' in this connotation of 'dog prison'. (Brock and Rankin, 2008, 31)

These three-year-old girls were often in roles from their favourite picture books: Carmen was a wicked stepmother chanting 'Mirror mirror on the wall', allocating her parents a role in her Sleeping Beauty; Katie when wearing a shawl would say 'I'm the poor, poor peasant woman' or 'I'm Red Riding Hood' and the 'Tiger came to tea' often at Melissa's house. (Brock and Rankin, 2008, 68)

Most children cannot escape literacy, as it permeates their environment and real-life settings – in their home, in nursery, on the television, in supermarkets and in the high street. They are surrounded by signs and notices in our highly literate environment and all young children will have everyday experiences with literacy. They will have received birthday cards, visited a favourite restaurant, observed electronic signs and digital screens, looked through catalogues, scribbled on pictures, and handled (and possibly chewed) packaging in the supermarket.

The early years librarian can help parents and carers to understand they are the best teachers to help their children to enjoy books and to get ready for learning to read. Learning occurs through interaction with what is available in the immediate environment and the caregiver's task is to provide the child with an enriched environment. Reading together and sharing books encourages talking, which helps develop speaking and listening skills. Fluent readers do well in school and reading and literacy skills will stand them in good stead for life in the 21st century.

Reading – making sense of those funny little squiggles

When we *can* read, we probably take being able to read for granted. One definition of reading is 'the cognitive process of understanding a written linguistic message'. Reading is a complicated process and learning to make sense of those funny squiggles on the page (as illustrated in Figure 1.2) involves a wide range of skills.

Figure 1.2   Sharing a story in the garden

Imagine that no-one had encouraged you to understand the funny little squiggles on the page called words that can make you gasp or can make you cry. You'd be a smaller person living in a smaller world. We believe that everyone deserves the right to those amazing moments that reading can bring us. And that we should all have more of them.

The Reading Agency website

The early years librarian is able to encourage an interest in reading by providing an environment of language and literacy through access to books, tapes, videos, computers, story and rhyme times, as well as a caring adult to introduce the child to literary pleasure.

Case study

A family visit to the library

Nathan (aged 6) and Callum (aged 5) visit the library with their mum.

Nathan always asks the library staff for help or information even though his mum is sitting there next to him. 'No mummy you don't know what to do. Let the lady do it.'

Tricia (Nathan and Callum's mum) observes: 'The librarians have a fantastic attitude to the children – very approachable, really friendly and always willing to help them. They promote a chatty, friendly and relaxed atmosphere. It's a great place. There are comfortable places to sit and read, bright displays and it's light and airy.

'I bring them here, but I'm not sure what they are getting out of it – that is to what level. I think that bringing them into this environment is very important. If they get used to it and when they go to secondary school, working in a library and handling books, accessing information from textbooks and doing homework won't be a problem for them. They will be comfortable in a library setting. My mum never ever took me to a library.

'You can go into Smiths and look at some books and buy the boys books, but look at the range of books that are here; you couldn't possibly buy them all. The whole concept is fantastic. Callum is fascinated by the non-fiction. I couldn't provide him with all this. These are the building blocks to set them up now for later life – using reference books and reading stories. This environment is great for Callum – he doesn't run around or shout – he has really calmed down here.'

Nathan, who is 'working' at the computer, but listening in on the discussion shouts: 'Callum hasn't calmed down!'

The above case study emphasizes Greene's (1991, 8) view that:

> The goals of the profession give librarians a vested interest in the child's development of language and reading skills. The librarian is interested in the preliterate development of the child, so in time there will be a reading child, and in still more time, a literate adult.

Early years librarians can foster emergent literacy by modelling reading and showing an interest and enjoyment in books. They can:

- provide opportunities for listening and following directions
- introduce sentences, words, letters and numbers
- introduce new vocabulary
- help children with story lines
- create social learning through group activities
- support discussion in story time (more about this in Chapters 5 and 6).

Early years librarians can suggest how parents can model reading and support their children by letting the children see them:

- enjoying reading and writing
- reading to themselves
- reading different things - poems, books, stories, messages, newspapers, instructions, advertisements
- writing for a range of purposes - notes, letters, lists, invitations, diary entries, filling in forms.

Modelling reading and writing is important, as is promoting a love of story and books. Encourage parents to read with and talk to their children about the books they are sharing, and to view the sharing and reading of books as an enjoyable experience. Here are a few pointers on how to support parents reading with children:

- encourage them to get their children to choose books for themselves
- be aware of what books and stories their children are likely to be interested in
- ask the early years practitioner for advice
- read with expression and intonation
- read familiar stories again and again
- give children time to look at pictures
- get children to participate in the storytelling
- encourage anticipation and prediction
- make connections to familiar experiences.

Get parents to demonstrate the reading process through showing their children:

- page or book layout
- left-to-right orientation
- turning the page in different directions
- scanning backwards and forwards for cues
- how texts and stories work
- the title, characters and content
- punctuation and what it's for.

There are, of course, issues here in relation to family literacy and the literacy levels of the parents themselves. Parents can be encouraged to improve their literacy levels by their own involvement in supporting their young children. This will be further explored in Chapter 2 when we look at partnerships with parents.

Reading as a social activity

Many people will view reading as a solitary activity, where the reader becomes privately absorbed in the place and time created for them by the author, or immersed in the detail of an information book. But reading can also be a very social activity, encouraging community involvement. Think of the current interest in reading groups and book clubs, and the initiatives promoted by The Reading Agency, which is an independent charity that aims to inspire more people to read more. Young children can certainly be socialized as they participate in reading as a social activity. This is very popular, judging by the number of rhyme time and story sessions offered in public libraries and other early years settings across the British Isles.

Reading has social benefits and the power to build relationships, according to a report from the National Literacy Trust (NLT, 2006). From the earliest act of parents sharing books with babies, to paired reading at school or grown-up reading groups, reading together can help form and nurture relationships. Research by the OECD (Kirsch, 2002) has shown that growing up in a home where reading is valued can have a greater effect on a child's achievement than parental wealth or education. The benefits of sharing books last longer than a lifetime, since a child who is brought up to value reading is likely to pass its love of reading - and good literacy skills - on to the next generation. Reading should be a pleasure; a love of the written word can take you into stories both real and fantasy, so that your own world is expanded and enriched.

Children need active and varied experiences to help master the complex skills involved in reading. They need to achieve through experience and success, as failure can lead to frustration and cause barriers to learning. Children try to make sense of their world and the learning process by using all strategies available, and this is the same for reading as for everything else they learn. They need to be interested, to be motivated, and they learn to achieve through building on early success. Practitioners encourage parents and carers to read aloud to their children from infancy and hold on to the idea that reading aloud is a shared social-bonding experience. Think about the different approaches that can be taken. It is far more positive for parents and carers to encourage the idea that reading is fun, as opposed to fulfilling the role of 'pushy parents', who are continually signalling the idea that reading is something that has to be worked hard at in order to achieve it.

Case study

A 'pushy parent'

Chloe's older sister learned to read easily and quickly worked her way through the reading scheme at nursery. When Chloe's turn came to attend nursery she showed very little interest in the reading scheme books. Mum was worried about her seeming lack of progress and tried using flash cards to hurry along the process. Chloe virtually ignored the flash cards, although she showed occasional flashes of involvement when Aunty provided bribes. Chloe eventually found her own route into reading – not that of her pushy parent.

Carolynn ('pushy parent') Rankin

Reading with children is a shared process, as the closeness of reading with an adult is special. Get parents to guide children to understanding and success without continually correcting them. Inform them that they are apprenticing children into reading. Get them to view it as a sharing time, rather than an instruction time. Encourage them to get their children to:

- make sense of the whole text
- talk about and understand what they are reading
- ask questions about the reading process
- see patterns in words and letters
- gain visual images of words
- use illustrations to help meaning
- match pictures to words
- use a variety of clues – if one doesn't work try another
- encourage their children to think 'Does that look right?' 'Does that sound right?' 'Does that make sense?'

Reading and storytelling activities in the early years library

Reading aloud to children is a well developed aspect of library provision. By providing quality children's books and holding activities and events, early years librarians can show by modelling how to read aloud to young children. The Reading Agency has produced *Hints for Reading to Under 5s*. Librarians may read straight through a book, whereas nursery teachers often interact with children by asking questions and encouraging questions. Using the technique of dialogic reading helps children to stay actively involved with a story and develop reading comprehension. Instead of reading the story straight through, ask open-ended questions about the story: 'Why do you think Goldilocks ate Baby Bear's porridge?' 'What do you think will happen next?'

- Are you confident enough to tell stories as well as read them? This takes more confidence and may require some practice; however the benefits can be enormous. You will probably feel empowered if you tell a story to an audience of enthralled young listeners. Start with something familiar such as *The Gingerbread Man* or *The Enormous Turnip*.
- Are you aware of the behavioural characteristics of your clientele and the implications of these for library services? For example, babies and toddlers may dribble and chew books, so materials and quality of resources are important. Babies and toddlers require space to move and crawl around and many settings now have cushions, bolsters, small comfy chairs and carpeted areas for them to explore in between handling the books.
- Do you provide activities for children to dress up and engage in role play? Many library settings now provide for play and developing of emergent literacy through role play. In addition to the books do you offer interesting materials, such as dressing up clothes, and musical instruments?
- Are you aware of the importance of active activities and enabling children to scribble and begin to write? Are there opportunities for children to draw, paint and be actively engaged in craft sessions

around story themes? Do you have crayons, paint, paper, card, envelopes, glue, clay, playdough, etc.? How do you cope with these resources in surroundings that cater for 'expensive' books?

Chapter 3 will explore designs for early years library settings, while Chapter 4 looks at the development of collections of resources, as well as books.

When planning for these experiences, don't just think about the resources, but also consider the communication, language and literacy demands. Through planning in this way other adults can become more focused on how to support children's experiences. You can encourage families to develop their own literacy and role-play experiences through the toys their children play with at home.

Young children's early years education should be a quality experience for all. Children learn most effectively through being involved in rich experiences and practical activities promoted through play; they learn through all their senses. Adults need to join in this play, both talking with and listening to the children, taking into account their interests and previous experiences.

Conclusion: helping to create positive experiences and memories in your library

How well prepared are you to ensure you can provide positive and enjoyable learning experiences for young children and their parents and carers? Katherine Ross suggests that one good way to think about the role of the reader is to think about your own experiences and reflect on your own reading history (Ross et al., 2006, 56). Were you read to as a child? Does your memory include a physical experience such as being bounced up and down to nursery rhymes? What can you remember about the first stages of reading on your own? Your professional practice, your partnership with parents and the activities and service offered in your library setting will shape the recollections and experiences of the next generation. We rather like that thought, and it sits comfortably with all the stuff about government policies, missions and targets.

Issues and questions

- How can you encourage families to use your library setting effectively?
- How can you model emergent reading and writing for children in meaningful ways?
- What do parents need to know about their children's literacy development?

Key points to remember

- Your role as an early years librarian is key.
- The UK political agenda has an impact on service provision.
- Working across disciplinary boundaries is important for professional practice.
- Reading to babies and young children is one of the most effective ways of encouraging early language.

Useful organizations

Booktrust, **www.booktrust.org.uk/home**
Bookstart, **www.bookstart.co.uk**
Chartered Institute of Library and Information Professionals (CILIP), **www.cilip.org.uk**
IFLA, **www.ifla.org**
National Literacy Trust, **www.literacytrust.org.uk**
Museums, Libraries and Archives Council (MLA), **www.mla.gov.uk**
Sure Start, **www.surestart.gov.uk**
The Reading Agency, **www.readingagency.org.uk**
Together for Children, **www.togetherforchildren.co.uk**
UNESCO, **www.unesco.org**

2

People and partnerships, skills and knowledge

Introduction

This chapter addresses the role of professionals in the interdisciplinary work involved in meeting the varied needs of the local community. It is particularly concerned with the roles of early years librarians and early years specialists as they seek to develop effective partnerships across the disciplines as well as foster partnerships with parents and carers. It considers how these professionals can provide quality, focused services and help to break down the barriers to those services that may be apparent in the community. Drawing on practice, the chapter also discusses the issues of developing effective communication and providing greater accountability to the stakeholders across the disciplines.

Communities give purpose to libraries and it is important that libraries seek to reach out to the local community beyond the library walls. Reading is an invaluable tool that can be used as the basis for connecting with various groups in society - babies and their families, looked-after children, young people at risk, the housebound as well as adults trying to improve literacy skills. Librarians and information workers share a critical value in that it is important to understand the needs of the user communities in order perform this task/function effectively and efficiently. Success in helping people to meet their information needs lies in understanding their difficulties and problems and is dependent on forming good working relationships. Young people are at the heart of the community. To increase their value, libraries can use community profiling to examine the needs of the target audience and determine how those needs can best be met. This may involve redefining the traditional role of the library as well as the traditional role of the librarian. The traditional children's department may need 'stretching' by expanding the age and scope of the target audience. For parents and carers, access to information and services during their children's early years is critical, particularly information about how everyday activities are linked to developing literacy and communication skills.

Libraries that invest in services for young children and their families increase the effectiveness of the provision. This should also have the secondary effect of helping to increase membership rates and loan records. Outreach work with diverse communities will encourage new cultural groups to use the service and will promote the library's role as a centre for the community. This represents an excellent opportunity to position the library as a partner in the development and education of young children. In addition, libraries that expand the role of children's services to include families may also be able to attract additional backing for their services and gain political support. As Feinberg and Feldman (1996, 2) write:

> In ranking or prioritizing services, public libraries would be loath to cut serv-
> ices to children even in an austerity budget. Service to children is essential,
> popular and an emotionally charged issue. Family centred services have the
> same cost benefit as children's services. They are essential, popular and emo-
> tionally or politically important services for all public or government institutions.
> Selecting family services as a role or strengthening children's services to
> include service to parents and agencies that serve parents, increases the polit-
> ical worth of the public library.　　　　　　　(Quoted in Feinberg et al., 2007)

The development of the new children's centre networks presents the opportunity to become an integral part of the multi-agency services provided. It also offers new avenues for reaching the young children of disadvantaged families in order to help make a difference to their speaking, listening, early reading and writing skills.

Case Study

Partnerships in Blackburn with Darwen

The Borough of Blackburn with Darwen in the north west of England was established in 1998 and has a culturally diverse population of 138,000. There are 13 children's libraries in Blackburn and Darwen and each one has an early years library. The library, along with the café, is seen as a key resource to draw in families. Our achievement depends on working in partnership and this was a major feature of our successful bid for Beacon status under the theme 'Libraries as a community resource'. We had to demonstrate our links with other departments and agencies, provide evidence of customer consultation and deliver outcomes linked to Borough targets. It's not always easy. Partnership working demands persistence, patience, participation and planning.

Jean Gabbatt, Literacy Development and Resources Manager,
Blackburn with Darwen

How to develop a family-friendly service – breaking down barriers to library use

It is vital to encourage families to use the library services. Remember, libraries are competing with the many other places that offer facilities and activities to families, so think carefully about how your library can offer something different. First consider the physical environment and the activities on offer. As a starting point, you could ask the staff to try to visualize the library from the customer's point of view. Familiarity can cause complacency. When working in the same place day in day out, we tend not to notice the little imperfections and begin to take the environment for granted. Perhaps it is a long time since we reflected on the layout of the furniture, or we may have failed to notice the out-of-date posters. Although the lighting is poor, and inadequate for either daytime or evening use, we have gradually become accustomed to it. Even the grumpy staff may have become accepted as part of the fittings and fixtures! It is important to challenge any complacency. Good negotiation skills may also prove to be essential, as you may need to convince management that staff time and resources used in evaluating a service or identifying a gap are time and effort well spent. Practitioners need to be aware of the library's customers and the needs of those customers.

Figure 2.1 A welcoming space

The library environment should be designed to create appropriate physical spaces and have appropriate furniture for the age group you are supporting. Thoughtful design using soft furnishings and child-friendly furniture will help to provide a welcoming location (as illustrated in Figure 2.1). We discuss space and design in more detail in Chapter 3.

Case study

The Sunshine Library

The innovative Sunshine Library, located in a community centre in Wakefield opened in 2001 and was the first early years library in the UK.

Designed with the help of parents, it has successfully removed traditional barriers to become a key social space in the local area. The Sunshine Library was purpose-built to support early language development and book enjoyment among families living in a deprived community. It was developed as a partnership between Sure Start, Wakefield Library and Information Service and Lupset Community Centre with additional funding from the Coalfield Regeneration Trust. Built as part of a local community centre the Sunshine Library is next door to a nursery school and a satellite library runs at the nearby Asian Women's Centre.

(Rankin et al., 2007)

How to provide a friendly service

Libraries can be good meeting places, providing a neutral, non-threatening environment – a place to share information with the community. We want to present a building that is encouraging and welcoming. However, thinking beyond the bricks and mortar, the human contact is also very important. Consider the library from your family users' point of view and how the staff interacts with them. Think about first impressions and how body language and non-verbal messages can either foster encouragement or show lack of interest and distain. Customer service is undoubtedly one of the most important areas for training and development in today's workplace. You might consider using recommended words or phrases to greet visitors. Review the signs and notices displayed around the library setting to ensure that your message is inclusive both culturally and from a gender perspective.

This is an opportunity for staff development. Leeds Library and Information Service are one of many authorities currently encouraging staff to undertake Frontline training and development. Frontline is an online course in reader-centred skills for library staff. Further details are available at **www.openingthebook.co.uk/frontline**. The training course is provided by Opening the Book, a company which specializes in reader development and library design and display. A customer-facing service will incorporate training into the daily work of the library service. Seek customer feedback on all aspects of your services. Consider how you can use analysis, self-assessment and observation to improve what is on offer.

Case study

Joining the library made easy

Many of our parents who use this [Sunshine] library would never go into a traditional library. There are many reasons why. They might have had a poor experience at school and not been interested in reading. They don't want to be judged on their parenting skills or lack of them, they just don't want anything official. Low literacy is a big issue in this community – if you can't read, you may question, 'What use is the library to me?' So we have lots of opportunities here, not challenges but opportunities. I had not been here long when I realized that the traditional offer of joining the library by completing a form was not a good option as many of our parents have poor literacy skills. I cannot tell when they walk through the door if they can read the form or not. So we changed our approach. Now when someone asks to join the Sunshine Library I say 'Of course you can. Sit down, have a drink and I'll fill your details in, just tell me your names and the children's dates of birth.' That was one change we brought in early on – you've got to break the barriers down.

Sunshine Librarian, Wakefield

Know your community – library standards and impact measures

In 2001 the government launched the *Public Library Service Standards* (*PLSS*) with the aim of creating a clear and widely accepted definition of the library authority's statutory duty to provide a comprehensive and efficient service. A third, revised edition of the *PLSS* was published by the Department for Culture, Media and Sport in June 2008 (DCMS, 2008). To guarantee the future role of libraries within local and national public service priorities it is vital to demonstrate the impact of library provision. As an additional level of accounting, the *Public Library Impact Measures* were implemented in April 2005 following extensive consultation and piloting with a range of library authorities. (MLA South East, 2007). They complement the revised *PLSS* and support the overall aims of *Framework for the Future*, the first-ever national public library strategy. The impact measures have been developed to demonstrate the value and influence public library services have on people and communities and include key activities in which all library authorities are expected to engage.

Community profiles

Library collections and services are shaped by the needs of the user community. Users are stakeholders, and identifying frequent users shows who the major stakeholders in the community are and which users form your current support base. Community profiles form the basis on which to identify the community needs for library services and facilities. A community profile provides a range of information about a group of people, usually based on their geographic location. The profile can include information on:

- population
- age
- ethnic groups
- religion
- health and care
- economic status
- households
- car ownership
- travel to work
- deprivation indicators
- demographic data
- library statistics.

Developing such profiles at authority and local ward level should help in the development of services. The intelligence you gather will inform planning, target setting and performance measurement, including impact measures. The measures should also be applicable at a local level, demonstrating how libraries are responding to local needs and priorities based on the results of community profiling. The process should also help to identify clients with special needs as a basis for designing and implementing services. Where there is an ethnically diverse community you will have information to support decision making on the resources and services to meet the needs of that community. Guidance on developing community profiles is provided by the Museums, Libraries and Archives Council, who set out the minimum level of information authorities should include. When undertaken periodically, community profiling can reflect the changing nature of the local community the library serves.

Assessing local needs

You will want to reach out so as to encourage potential users to access your services. Library users are created by involving parents. You can use profiles of customers and potential customers to develop good services. General developmental information can be gathered for children, recognizing the development needs of young children – developmental stages include language levels, mobility, emotional maturity, communication skills and social development. Think about and be aware of how customers use their time in your early years library setting. Are there any ethnic or cultural time factors that you can use to encourage visits, for example, celebrating particular holidays and festivals? Actually getting to your library may also be an issue if families are dependent on local public transport or if there is nowhere to park the car. The events and holidays happening as part of the school calendar will be important from a family-visit viewpoint. Think about the family constraints.

Case study

Significant outcomes of the early years library provision in Wakefield

We have numerous examples of the significant impact our Early Years Librarians have made on the lives of many young children and their parents, in areas where literacy levels are particularly low:

- Approximately 95% of families using our Early Years Library have never used libraries before and perceptions of books, reading and learning are being positively changed.
- As disadvantaged young children develop a love of books and stories, literacy skills are being established.
- Families without access to computers in the home, children and parents, have developed IT skills in a non-threatening environment, either to access information or to assist with CVs and job applications.
- Professional help has enabled parents to enrol on IT/Basic Skills training courses, or take a leading role in the community through fund-raising, chairing meetings, volunteering within the Sure Start community and successfully gaining employment.
- Children with little or no confidence and poor communication skills have started to interact at story sessions and developed new social skills in the friendly environment.
- Families who feel isolated, including Asian families, asylum seekers and Travellers have discovered a safe, non-threatening environment in which to access support with literacy and information.
- Parents and children have had a significant involvement in the development of the service.
- Where families have needed additional support from other agencies, librarians have been able to assist with the referral process.

Cath Threapleton, Principal Cultural Officer:
Children and Social Cohesion, Wakefield

Developing effective partnerships – with other professionals and partner organizations

Library and information practitioners have a tradition of networking with other professional groups and developing communities of practice. Working in early years provision, you are most likely to be involved in a multi-professional team made up of representatives from different professional groups or involving members from different organizations. Sullivan and Skelcher (2002) highlight the rise in collaborative working between public, business, and voluntary and community sectors – collaboration is now central to the way in which public policy is made, managed and delivered in the UK. Funding and the authority for the development and delivery of public policy are increasingly located in collaborative ventures involving a range of governmental, business, voluntary and community agencies. This is the bigger picture discussed in Chapter 1 and as a player in a multidisciplinary team your story time sessions fit into the increasingly complex landscape of early years provision in the UK. This is why the role of the early years librarian is so important. Partnership working is seen as an important strategy for tackling complex issues such as social inclusion and supporting the lifelong learning agenda. Many workplace settings now require the delivery of services or projects by a series of teams, each one a multidisciplinary team made up of a range of different professionals. This presents particular challenges for the team leaders in a complex work environment. Staff in the same teams may be employed under different contractual arrangements and line-managed by different managers working in different agencies, each with its own operating procedures and practices. The following experience of a Sure Start librarian highlights this:

> Partnership work is fantastic most of the time. When I initially started with Sure Start they tried to give me three line managers so I said 'Can I just have one please!' We have Sure Start targets to reach and library targets to reach. Instead of me having two performance appraisals, one with the library manager and one with the Sure Start programme manager, we eventually arranged for me to have one appraisal with both managers present. That makes much more sense but it took a year to achieve this.
>
> Sure Start librarian

Partnership working can present challenges and barriers, particularly in cross-sector partnerships where participants can often have different strategic priorities and work to different time frames. Rankin et al. (2007) found that the early years librarians in their Wakefield case-study area were achieving very successful results in the services they offered and the varied outreach activities provided, but the funding for their posts was from non-core sources and a potential complication for sustainability was that they were not directly line-managed by the public library service. Some of the challenges associated with this type of multidisciplinary team work are discussed further in Chapter 6, where we look at projects and planning.

A key message here is that librarians can play an important role as connectors, working in inter-organizational teams. Networking with other organizations can provide the early years library practitioner with information about other services that are available to families, and this will enhance your role as an information provider and referral agent. Through effective partnerships there is also evidence of other professionals acting as advocates for early years library provision. For example, Sawyer, Pickstone and Hall (2007) evaluated the promotion of speech and language in 15 Sure Start local programmes. One of their key findings mentions collaboration with early year librarians – using books to promote language skills and develop an interest in books. A recommendation is that the contribution of early years librarians should be examined and developed further.

Case study

Partnership work in action – successful referral

Adam, aged 3, came regularly to the story time sessions in The Rainbow Library. His mum was worried about his speech and language development and his behaviour. She eventually felt confident enough to speak to the early years librarian about her concerns. Through the local partnership's record keeping and information sharing, the librarian made a referral to the family support team and the family now has the needed speech therapy support. The early years library staff are also working with Adam in the group activity sessions to improve his speech and his attitude to others.

Rainbow Librarian, Airedale Library and Family Centre, Castleford

Good management and leadership skills are important and early years librarians need not only to work in a team with the other librarians but also to promote ongoing discussion and negotiation with members of staff in other services. It is important to have an understanding of your parent organization's strategy and business plan and to be able to implement decisions.

The effective practitioner will develop good political and advocacy skills. Remember, an advocate is a person who publicly supports or recommends a particular cause or policy. A key part of your work will be to develop co-operative programmes with other agencies. This may also involve developing policies and procedures applying to children's services on the basis of current legislation.

Case study

Partnership work – co-operating with other agencies

A young mum who regularly attended Once Upon a Rhyme with her toddler and baby stopped coming. I was concerned because I knew there was a history of post-natal depression. I contacted her and she came in to the library and asked to speak to me. After she explained what she had been experiencing, I suggested that we made a referral to the Family Support team. A care package was put together which included some respite care for the children. She is now recovering. Allowing her time to catch up with sleep and professional help through her GP was all she needed to regain her strength and self-worth.

Rainbow Librarian, Airedale Library and Family Centre, Castleford

The early years librarian will need skills beyond a love of books and children, as a key part of your role is serving the whole family as opposed to only the child.

Partnerships – encouraging parents and carers to get involved

Children's centres are key to encouraging parents to get actively involved in their children's early learning, which we know can impact positively on children's attainment when they reach school. A key part of your role is to promote active partnerships with parents and to communicate effectively with families. Babies and young children cannot visit your library setting on their own – they need to be brought there by a parent or carer. You need to encourage that adult to visit and to engage with the resources and services you have on offer. Many may be easily put off by their own early experience of using a library; maybe they have never used one. Even the name 'library' in a children's centre may be off-putting to some adults. As an effective practitioner, treat parents as partners. White reminds us that 'Librarians have the great advantage of having a relationship with a parent or care-giver that is voluntary and based on mutual trust and respect; a partnership where both are dedicated to achieving the best for the child' (2002, 17). You may not be able to have a one-to-one impact on babies or young children, but you should maximize the opportunity to influence their primary carers.

Case study

Local community involvement in the local library

Parents and children were actively involved throughout the planning and development of the Sunshine Library and were consulted during the drafting of the plans. They helped select stock and loan materials, furniture and equipment. They were involved in choosing the farmyard theme for the library interior and the 'Sunshine' name for the library.

'Over the five years that the services have been operating [professional library] staff have developed services to meet local needs – it is impossible to have a "one-size-fits all service".'   Sunshine Librarian, Wakefield

Wakefield Library and Information Services has proactively developed the role of volunteers by encouraging parental involvement in decisions about service development and in helping with routine tasks within the early years libraries and the children's centres. Parent volunteers have always been encouraged in the running of the Sunshine Library and it has been an important channel for helping individuals develop new skills and gain confidence. A number of parent volunteers have gone on to paid employment and to full-time education. In order to continue this good practice across the children's centres, an effective volunteer training package is being developed in the authority.

Case study

Transforming your library by involving the community – ideas from the Love Libraries campaign

The following example from the Love Libraries campaign highlights opportunities for local people to be involved in helping to transform their local library. The campaign began in March 2006, and as part of the launch three public libraries were transformed and refurbished over a period of 12 weeks, using ideas from local people. New services were introduced to attract more people in the community. The layout of Richmond Library was totally redesigned. Coldharbour Library in Gravesend, Kent, had a makeover to create a much lighter, airier feel. The entrance was opened up into a quick-choice books area and the huge counter was replaced by two small borrowing pods. Geometric flooring and visual features like red sofas and a comfy reading den were designed to entice people into the different areas. The library at Newquay in Cornwall underwent a complete overhaul of design and layout, using colourful visuals with a local sea theme and better lighting to create a welcoming and relaxing atmosphere. The barriers and counter at the entrance were replaced by quick book choice and comfy reading areas with coffee, newspapers and magazines. You can read more about these projects at www.lovelibraries.co.uk/libraries.php.

Parents have the best understanding of their own children and you can use this knowledge to help provide resources and services to meet the children's needs. When parents support their children's literacy they make much better progress. These early experiences make such a difference to children's later achievements. Encourage parents to read and write with their children at home and advocate their supporting and being part of their children's literacy development. However, do advise against over-pressuring their child. The child's enjoyment and motivation are of utmost importance. You could think about organizing literacy workshops for parents, or invite them in to support and be part of children's learning through play.

Parents and carers are in the best position to help young children get ready to read, as in the following guidance:

1 Young children have short attention spans. You can do activities for short bits of time throughout the day.
2 Parents know their children best and can help them learn in ways and at times that are easiest for them.
3 Parents are tremendous role models - if your children see that you value and enjoy reading, they will follow your lead.
4 Children learn best by doing things - and they love doing things with YOU. So read with your children every day.

Interactions that occur between young children and their carers are important as they not only promote close relationships and early language development but also contribute to children's intellectual development. Practitioners in close contact with parents, such as health visitors and childcare workers are in a good position to support and encourage parents. This includes you as the early years library practitioner, as you can all work together to suggest ways in which parents and their young children can begin the early literacy journey together.

Understanding the information needs of parents

Although we have been focusing on the needs of young children, their parents and carers are also adult learners with their own individual needs. People do not always know what information needs they have and some parents may not feel confident about asking questions. They may not know that they have an information gap, or may be unwilling to recognize it. Despite being in the very best position to introduce their children to literacy, many parents lack the confidence and knowledge to fulfil the role of their baby's first educator. According to Nicholas (2000), there are many factors involved in the meeting of information needs including occupation, cultural background, the personality of the individual, and level of awareness and training. Time, access to available resources, costs and information overload will also play a part. The early years practitioner should have a good knowledge of the client group – children and their families. To effectively support this community you should have an understanding of the theory of children's learning and the implications for the provision of library services. By providing support for parents through a parenting collection and referral services you are encouraging a family-friendly library environment. To enable effective communication with parents and carers it is helpful to keep the following guidelines in mind (adapted from Feinberg, Deerr et al., 2007, 87-8):

Anticipate that parents will ask questions

Be ready to deal with enquiries of a sensitive nature and know how to provide referral information to partner professionals in the family support team. It is important for support staff in the library setting to be aware of partner organizations.

Give advice based on qualifications and experience

It is important to remember that an early years librarian is not a personal friend, counsellor or social worker. There is a fine line between providing information and offering advice. Your role is to offer professional support to the family as opposed to assuming the role of being a personal friend. Know when to refer to others who are qualified to help.

Be approachable but draw boundaries

You cannot solve all problems, but use listening skills to determine what the parent actually wants. Ask pertinent questions so that you can refer parents to the appropriate agency for help or make the contact on their behalf. Personal boundaries are also important.

Become familiar with local resources and family support services, as parents in need may need information quickly.

A study commissioned by the National Evaluation of Sure Start (NESS) describes how involving parents can be very empowering. The investigation used six Sure Start case-study areas to take a closer look at parents' experiences of empowerment and the types of mutual support and community action that had been developed. The researchers 'found substantial evidence for experiences of individual parent empowerment' (Williams and Churchill, 2006, 5). Parents in the study expressed the value of Sure Start in terms of increased confidence, skills and self-esteem as parents. One factor that influenced the opportunities for empowerment involved transforming professional relationships with parents. Williams and Churchill (2006) note that many parents commented that Sure Start staff treated them differently from other professionals in the health, education and welfare services; this involved being welcoming, friendly, supportive and non-judgemental. The study also found that when Sure Start local programmes provided responsive, accessible, available and inclusive services this also enhanced parents' access to resources. This involved dedicated outreach work, flexible times and locations for activities and regular information in the community, targeted at those with and without English language skills (2006, 7). Empowering local communities was also an element, and this meant that teams needed to have community development skills as well as family support and health-related expertise. Although the NESS study did not specifically involve library services, these findings echo the evidence gathered by the early years librarians in the Wakefield early years libraries.

More positive outcomes from the Sunshine Library

I really don't know what I would have done without the Sunshine, I really don't know how I would have coped. Nobody knew how depressed I was – it was the only place I could face coming to.

Mum who has a child with Down's syndrome

Libraries like the Sunshine should be accessible to all communities. The long-term problems resulting from low literacy levels could be vastly reduced if the first experiences of books and reading materials were like those available to the lucky children living in the Wakefield West Sure Start area.

Local parent

Early years librarians can create opportunities for communication and develop relationships with parents. This can be done in an informal way by involving parents in interactive story sessions, or inviting them to help with puppet shows. Some early years settings have very successfully involved parents in designing and making story sacks based around themes of interest to the local community. You are creating library users by involving parents. Early years librarians will be well positioned to talk to local people about what services they might like, and to gather views on what is already available. Consider the potential barriers involved in local community use and be brave about considering changes. You may need to challenge the 'usual way' of doing something.

In some locations there is also the challenge of how to communicate with parents who are working long hours or are simply very busy. They may not know about your services or not be able to access the library because of restricted opening times. Consider how they can be encouraged to visit to your library setting and get involved in activities with their young children. Families are all different and children may live with one or both parents, with carers or with other relatives in an extended family. Ask parents for their views on your services. One way of encouraging contact is to display lists of greetings words in English and other languages. You can then invite parents and families to contribute and add to the display. As an effective practitioner you should value each child's culture and you can help them to make connections between experiences at home, at the library and in the whole community. See the Sure Start *Toolkit for Reaching Priority and Excluded Families* (Sure Start, 2007).

Involving fathers

So far we have discussed parents and families getting involved with supporting early literacy and in making library visits, yet more often than not it is the mums who are involved. It is equally important that fathers have access to similar opportunities to interact with their babies and form close relationships through playing, chatting, singing songs and telling stories with them. They also have a part to play in promoting early language skills. You can select books which promote good father figures as well as good mother figures, and plan to hold events at times when fathers are most likely to be able to attend. Staff in early years settings (children's centres and libraries) tend to be predominantly female. This makes it doubly important that fathers get involved whenever possible to act as positive role models. Research findings by the Pre-school Learning Alliance on fathers' involvement in early years settings highlighted the growing awareness of the important role fathers play in their children's learning and development. It is a key component of the inclusion agenda advocated by government and other organizations and agencies (Kahn, 2005). Reaching and engaging fathers is one of the core aims of children's centres and the challenge is to get fathers involved even before their baby is born. The government has published plans to make children's centres and other public services more father inclusive. *Aiming High for Children: supporting families*, a joint HM Treasury and Department for Education and Skills document (*Aiming High for Children*, 2007) linked to government spending plans for 2008-11, promises extra support for resident and non-resident dads to help them play their critical role in children's development.

The National Literacy Trust has produced a publication aimed at professionals who work with parents, *Getting the Blokes on Board: involving fathers and male carers with their children*, which contains ideas for getting dads and male carers reading with their children (NLT, 2007a).

Some Top Tips for engaging dads

Children are often the biggest motivator – give dads the opportunity to do something with or for their children.

Use the mums – many mums act as 'gatekeepers' for their childrens' education, so involve them in encouraging dads to get on board.

Timing – as dads may be more likely to be at work during the day, think about other times when they might be available, such as early mornings, evenings or weekends.

Know your background – be persistent, creative, patient and sensitive in the recruitment of fathers.

They like to do something, not talk about it. Use hands-on, activity-based sessions.

Plan for long term commitment – don't worry about numbers as word of mouth will help if you are successful.

Speak to them directly – events labelled 'for parents' tend to attract mothers. Address letters to fathers and try other communication routes like text messages and e-mails.

Consult – ask fathers for their advice on publicity, recruitment, timings, activity themes.

Remember that not all dads are the same.

Look at the whole organization's attitude – you only have one chance to make a first impression and that needs to be a positive experience.

Allow time for staff training and discussion of the issues around encouraging dads to bring their babies and young children into the early years library.

Adapted from 'Top Tips for Engaging Dads'. In *Getting the Blokes on Board* (2007, 6, online)

Five Minutes

The 'Five Minutes' promotion, 'It takes five minutes to shave - it takes five minutes to read to your child', is aimed at fathers with lower levels of literacy. This campaign from The Vital Link actively promotes libraries as the place where dads can discover books to share with their children. This supports any work you are doing with families and The Vital Link project, through encouraging adults to get into reading. It includes display materials and dedicated booklists for libraries, family centres, children's centres and schools. Further information is available on The Vital Link website, **www. literarytrust.org.uk/vitallink**.

Involving grandparents

In today's busy society, where the vast majority of mums are out at work during the day, many grandparents have an important role in childcare and have regular contact with their grandchildren. Grandparents can make a huge contribution to the lives of their grandchildren and to their learning and development. This is potentially a large group of the population, who form an important part of children's support network. There is an emotional bond between children and their grandparents. Grandparents have the experience to exercise particular patience in listening to young children. They can be encouraged to tell their stories and share their experiences in library storytelling sessions (as illustrated in Figure 2.2). The *Communicate with your Grandchild* pack has been developed by Talk To Your Baby in conjunction with the Grandparents' Association. It recognizes the important role that grandparents play in the development of their grandchildren's communication and language skills. The pack contains ideas for grandparents on talking to children in everyday situations, sharing books together and enjoying nursery rhymes and music.

Figure 2.2   Grandfather and grandson sharing a story

The home learning environment

What parents and carers do makes a real difference to young children's development. The EPPE (Sylva et al., 2004) project developed an index to measure the quality of the home learning environment. This measures a range of activities that parents undertake with pre-school children that are related to improvements in children's learning and have a positive effect on their development. For example, reading to children, teaching songs and nursery rhymes, painting and drawing, playing with letters and numbers, visiting the library, teaching the alphabet, teaching numbers, taking children on visits and creating regular opportunities for them to play with their friends at home were all associated with higher intellectual and social/behavioural scores.

The My Home Library website has printable bookplates that can be downloaded and put in favourite books (**www.myhomelibrary.org/home. html**). Mums can be encouraged to stick them in the baby's first picture books. You can suggest that families write a thank-you note or a birthday card together. Another idea is to set up a home library with some favourite books on a special shelf.

More times for book sharing

Encourage parents to set aside a special time each day, such as nap time, bedtime, or after meals. It is better to share books when parent and child are both in a relaxed mood. Reading together at bedtime is not only important for creating settled routines and listening to stories, it is also key in forming close, warm and sharing relationships. Parents can also take advantage of 'waiting' times to share books – on trips, at the health centre, waiting at the bus stop or queuing at the supermarket checkout. Reading even 5 or 10 minutes a day to young children helps them get ready to read on their own.

Reaching families with low literacy – The Vital Link approach

Run by The Reading Agency in partnership with the National Literacy Trust, The Vital Link focuses on how creative reading activities organized by libraries can motivate students and engage new learners. The aim of The

Vital Link is for emergent readers and adults with low literacy levels to benefit from a consistently high-quality reading service offered by public libraries working in partnership with Skills for Life providers. Having a child is a life-changing event and it can inspire parents to do many things – sometimes things that they have been putting off for a while. Reading can be something that parents become more motivated to do after their children are born. Got kids? Get reading!™ is a Vital Link project for adults who are not confident readers and have children aged seven and under. The Vital Link has produced promotional packs for libraries, family centres, schools and others working with parents with low levels of literacy and its website includes lots of support for librarians and adult literacy professionals who want to work together. This includes toolkits, case studies of successful collaborations, training information and First Choice Books, a database of books suitable for adults who aren't confident readers.

Case study

'Picture This' in Blackburn with Darwen

The 'Picture This' project was designed to encourage adults with basic literacy skills to share books with their children. It can be embarrassing for people to admit to poor reading skills but this can be avoided by using picture books and encouraging parents and carers to share them with their children. Reading proficiency isn't necessary when using picture books, as the illustrations usually tell the stories. This type of scheme only works with help from parents. One of the achievements in this particular area was to encourage local families to attend a series of themed sessions.

This chapter has looked at how early years librarians can be involved in partnerships with other professionals and with parents and local communities. A key aim is to develop family-friendly services and the next chapter will consider the importance of the library environment in creating a welcoming atmosphere.

Issues and questions

- How can you develop and maintain partnerships with other key professionals, community organizations, parents and the extended family?
- How can you promote a welcoming ethos and provide a family-friendly service?
- Are you able to develop your community profile and so meet service and impact standards?

Key points to remember

- Setting and meeting targets is an important part of the librarian's role.
- Providing effective services by knowing local community needs makes a real difference.
- Partnership working demands persistence, patience, participation and planning.

Useful organizations

Chartered Institute of Library and Information Professionals (CILIP), **www.cilip.org.uk**

Grandparents' Association, **www.grandparents-association.org.uk**

Museums, Libraries and Archives Council (MLA) (for standards), **www.mla.gov.uk**

National Literacy Trust, **www.literacytrust.org.uk**

Opening the Book, **www.openingthebook.com**

Pre-school Learning Alliance, **www.pre-school.org.uk**

Sure Start, **www.surestart.gov.uk**

Talk to Your Baby, **www.literacytrust.org.uk/talktoyourbaby**

Together for Children, **www.tda.gov.uk**

The Vital Link, **www.literacytrust.org.uk/vitallink**

3

Buildings, design and space

Introduction

This chapter addresses the role of the library building as an important place in the community. It also considers the environment and design of the space within the early years library. It is important to create a welcoming atmosphere and the ambience, layout, design, furniture and fittings will have a part to play. We will encourage you to think about how you use colour, and how the books and resources are displayed. The design approaches that libraries have used will be discussed. We will consider what makes for a good design in an early years library and suggest how you negotiate with architects and designers to achieve this.

Since the government's Better Public Building initiative was launched (CABE, 2003) we have seen high-quality building design result in some outstanding new schools, libraries, hospitals and transport infrastructure. Too many new public buildings, however, still fall short of the high standards expected. Improved public buildings with good design provide a better environment for staff and, more importantly, for the members of the public who make use of the services and facilities. To ensure that your library provides the best possible environment for the babies, children and adults who patronize it, it is important to take the time to consider the most appropriate and user-friendly layout, structure and design of the building.

A well designed building has a greater value to all involved:

> Architecture and design does matter – it communicates identity and values. A sense of place encourages social cohesion. It is a vital part of quality of life.
>
> (David Lammy, Culture Minister, speaking in 2006)

Why should early years librarians be concerned about architecture and design?

The question inevitably arises: why should early years librarians be concerned about architecture and design? You may well be thinking: 'I'm only involved as part of the team delivering services once the building is already constructed. The design issues are the concern of senior managers.' However, the current trend for multi-disciplinary teamwork means that you could have the unique opportunity to have input into a new project and be part of designing a building that suits the purpose you have in mind. Avoid being involved in the design and planning of the early years library, and the result could be the creation of an area that you find unsatisfactory and unsuitable for your requirements. Architects and designers can have excellent ideas, but their priorities may differ from yours in terms of what is important in layout and use of space. You are the expert regarding what is necessary, practical and desirable in the early years library. As recognized by the Commission for Architecture and the Built Environment (CABE), you are the one left behind after the designers and planners have all moved on, and it is important that you are happy with the end result.

Case study

The shrinking library!

The library kept shrinking! This was happening during the design and planning stage of our first children's centre library and the room size was eventually cut down to the minimum.

There was much negotiation and we had to take a cut on the potential staffing, but the library was included and we now have a very successful

children's centre library. So my advice is: never miss a planning meeting –
the librarian's voice needs to be heard!

Jean Gabbatt, Literacy Development and Resources Manager,
Blackburn with Darwen

It may be that you are a member of a multi-disciplinary team planning a
purpose-built setting in a children's centre, or you are involved in
refurbishment in a public library setting. Perhaps you have been appointed
to a new position and have inherited an existing children's library, or maybe
you just want to take a fresh look at the current provision in your area.
Whatever the scenario, it can be beneficial to have a regular review of the
use of the spaces provided for babies and young children and their families.

First impressions – the challenge

First impressions count! Consider this challenge. Try to imagine what your
existing library setting seems like to first-time visitors. You may think it has
a friendly, lively, busy and vibrant ambience, with everything clearly laid out
using a carefully designed system. There may be lots of notices and posters,
possibly in several different languages. Perhaps there are leaflet dispensers
overflowing with free information about events, opportunities and activities
on offer, or hundreds of colourful picture books displayed in 'kinder boxes'.
Nevertheless, to the anxious parent who has never used a library before and
to her 18-month-old child it may all seem quite overwhelming. The
grandparent who remembers being told to keep quiet in a library as a
youngster may not even consider visiting with his boisterous grandchildren.

The first impression children and parents gain from an early years
library is its entrance and reception area. How well does yours measure up;
are visitors' first impressions likely to generate a positive experience? If you
are involved in a brand new build or a refurbishment project, try to imagine
what the ideal early years library should look like and how it should feel
to the users. Libraries of various sizes and types are realizing the positive
impact of creating comfortable and welcoming library environments for
patrons of all ages. For years, school and public libraries have drawn in the
very young and their parents with creative, enticing children's areas.

According to Lushington (2002), a library should be easy to find, easy to enter and easy to use.

The library as a community space

Consider the library as a community space. There is a strongly held view that libraries offer a welcoming, neutral space that provides opportunities for personal, cultural and community development in appropriate circumstances (Harris and Dudley, 2005, 18). Do you agree with this statement? Does it reflect your library setting? Recent research by MORI (2003) demonstrates the impact of the built environment on our quality of life. Homes, schools, surgeries, streets and parks combine to form the 'physical capital' of a local area. If we are concerned about improving quality of life then we must focus more attention on the design quality of our urban fabric. Policy makers have been focusing on the importance of social capital, deprivation and cohesion over the last few years, and the evidence suggests that we should also be paying attention to the very structure and nature of the places we are creating (MORI, 2003, 3).

There is currently a huge amount of building in progress to provide multi-agency centres and integrated children's centres. Partnership programmes are important and libraries can help to build social capital by providing a safe place for people to meet, socialize and relax. The emotional environment in a setting is created by all the people involved, both young and old. However, it is up to the adults to ensure that it is warm and welcoming to everyone. The adults need to empathize with children and support their emotions. The children's library should be homely enough to feel comfortable while fulfilling the needs of the wider service. This may be a particularly difficult challenge in a shared-use area in a public library where the children's area is next to adult provision.

> The beauty of having a library that is targeted at young children is that you can have the right staff, you can decorate it, you can target to the families; whereas usually in our libraries we are trying to do all things for everybody and have difficulty in attracting all the age groups.
>
> Senior library manager

The importance of the environment and space

The physical appearance and location of buildings have an impact on the local community, but the environment inside is also important. As we look at the practical aspects of designing library space for very young children, let's start by considering some environmental factors. The childcare expert Friedrich Froebel (1782-1852) stressed the importance of environmental space. Froebel's view was that the first learning experiences of the very young are of crucial importance in influencing not only their later educational achievements but also the health and development of society as a whole.

Froebel devised a set of principles and practices which would form part of an interactive educational process to take place in institutions which, in 1840, he named 'kindergärten'. These principles also provide good advice when considering the design of early years library provision. *Elements of a Froebelian Education for Children from Birth to Seven Years* includes recognition of the uniqueness of each child's capacity and potential and of the importance of play as a central integrating element in a child's development and learning. This pedagogy involves parents, carers and educators working in harmony and partnership. Froebel proposed an environment which is physically safe but intellectually challenging, promoting curiosity, enquiry, sensory stimulation and aesthetic awareness and which allows free access to a rich range of materials that promote open-ended opportunities for play, representation and creativity (**www.froebel.org.uk/elements.html**).

The late Anita Rui Olds was a noted designer and psychologist with 30 years of experience in the design of children's environments. She felt that much emphasis is placed on the visual aspects of architecture, but it is really the feeling of buildings and our sense of either well-being or 'dis-ease' when we are in them that is at the roots of the architectural experience (2001, 22). She was the founder and director of The Child Care Institute, an annual training programme helping architects, designers and childcare providers to design spaces.

Environment as the third teacher – the Reggio Emilia approach

Environments can play a crucial part in the ethos of a setting and can be a key factor in ideologies behind education, care or services. Northern Italy is home to the Reggio Emilia programme of early childhood education, which has gained an international reputation since the first schools were started by parents in 1945 in the aftermath of the Second World War. It is now a city-run, sponsored system designed for all children from birth through six years of age. The Reggio Emilia approach recognizes the environment as the third teacher – parents and carers being the other two. Great attention is given to the look and feel of the early years setting. Space is organized for small and large group projects and small, intimate spaces for one, two or three children. Displays are at both adult and children's eye level and the furniture is designed to be multifunctional. Reggio settings make marked use of natural and artificial light, with floor-to-ceiling windows and pale walls that set off the colourful artwork done by the children. The outside environment is also a source of colour and texture and plants are widely used in the classroom as well as in interior courtyards. (Community Playthings, 2006)

In another example, the Steiner early childhood settings give careful consideration to the impact of everything in the kindergarten environment upon all the senses of a young child. There are no 'hard' corners, no strong colours and all the furniture and toys are made of natural materials. Started by Dr Rudolf Steiner (1861–1925) in Stuttgart in 1919, the philosophy of Steiner schools is to promote universal human values and provide holistic education for children of all abilities, ethnicities and religions. Even some of the equipment is made out of natural resources, such as beeswax (for crayons) and sheep's fleece.

Architecture and design – planning and designing spaces for the children's libraries of the future

It is important to try to visualize the environment through a child's eyes. Consider the following challenge:

Get down on the floor and move around at child level. If you lie on your back and look up (a baby's perspective), you will realise that even ceilings are relevant!

Community Playthings (2006)

Anita Olds (2001) has identified five factors which contribute to a truly great room layout, to a design that guides and encourages children to learn through play.

1   Location – where is it in relation to other physical features and other activity areas?
2   Boundaries – how well is the area defined?
3   Variety – is there enough to keep the children interested?
4   Storage – the materials children need in each activity area should be stored conveniently at hand, and displayed attractively for effective use.
5   Mood – is the mood of the area appropriate to the function? Is it home like?

Olds (2001) also reminds us that decisions involving functions, budgets and materials performance are improved when people knowledgeable in these areas contribute their experience and expertise to the design. We should ask architects and contractors to provide cost estimates for alternative designs and materials. It would be good to see models and mock-ups of areas so that staff can evaluate the three-dimensional aspects of a space. You can role-play the use you plan to make of each space so as to test out the requirements. A collaborative process encourages people to think about how we are currently doing things and how we would really like to be doing them in the future. In making suggestions about early years library provision, don't be constrained by repeating what you may already have – consider innovation.

Design is important

The Commission for Architecture and the Built Environment (CABE) was set up in 1999 as the government's design champion. Funded through central government, it aims to promote the role of quality design in new buildings and produces a range of publications on planning and design. Well designed spaces are cheaper to manage and better cared for by the people who use them. Doing design well requires more than an understanding of aesthetics - looks are important but the usefulness of the end product is what is really important.

Design champions – is there one in your organization?

Delivering design quality requires strong leadership. The government has called for all public bodies with a responsibility for delivering and managing the built environment to appoint a 'design champion'. CABE is leading on this initiative and wants to see design champions deployed in every local authority in England. While the role of a design champion will vary from organization to organization, their purpose is to provide leadership and motivation, ensuring a clear vision and strategy for delivering good design. An effective design champion will promote the benefits of good design, support and challenge colleagues to be good clients and inspire others to in turn champion good design themselves. Is there a design champion in your organization? This person can prove invaluable during the design process.

The role of the client – consultation opportunities

A well designed building is one that contributes to the business, is suitable for its intended use and is built to last. As an early years librarian you may be asked to be part of a project team working alongside other specialists in the development of a new centre, or make contributions to planning discussions. Either way, you will need to interact with the architects and designers commissioned to develop the plans. Architects generally seek staff input initially but may not always check out the consequences of design solutions later on. The client role is very important in the design and build partnership. To be a successful client you can look at other early years building projects to get ideas, and talk to people involved in similar projects about their experiences. Another important aspect is to commit to sustainability (CABE 2003). Consultation with the user community is important. Mark Dudek, an architect specializing in design for young children advises that:

> Buildings should not merely satisfy basic needs, they should provide the right amount and kind of space for activities that will interest and stimulate their users. Most good architecture combines the practical with something less tangible; a sense of delight in the spaces which make up a building as a whole, which may even modify the moods of its users in a positive way. If designed skilfully, a building will help to make children's experience of their early years care a secure yet varied one.
>
> (2001, 8)

When discussing the design of the early years library setting with the architect, it is important to be clear about what you want. Dudek continues: 'Early years practitioners often ask architects to create a "homely" setting – a subjective and imprecise term that could mean all sorts of different things. It is vital that reflection about form and style go beyond this basic kind of definition.' The architect needs to know how the building will be used, who the clients will be, its purpose and how it will complement its surroundings. Once he/she has this broad picture in mind, it would be helpful, where possible, to include parents and children in the discussions so as to allow the architect to fill in the details. It will enable the architect to gain a better understanding of the project and the direction will be set to ensure that it starts off on the right footing. Dudek concludes, 'It is crucial that the architect or architectural practice selected to oversee the project is in tune with your needs, willing to be flexible and to take your views and those of the community seriously' (2001, 77).

It is really important to have an understanding of what you want to achieve before meeting an architect or design team. Things that are really important to you may not be included in the final design brief, so be well prepared and assertive in stating your requirements. As stated earlier, architects will consult with clients to establish needs, but requests are not always followed through. Listed below are some design stage considerations that you can raise with the architect. Although directed at those specifically involved in nursery provision, many of these points will be helpful at design stage when discussing requirements for the early years library setting:

- a central common area, with rooms opening from it, is preferable to corridors
- mobile storage is preferable to built-in storage
- direct access from playroom to outdoor play area
- nappy-changing unit and toilet facilities should be easily accessible from indoor and outdoor play areas
- doors: keep to a minimum, as they take space and generate traffic
- windows: natural light is excellent, and children love to look out; but too much glass creates a harsh environment, takes valuable wall space, and makes us feel exposed
- floor surfaces: consider safety (non-slip), ease of cleaning, sound absorption, and visual effect
- ceiling surfaces: acoustic tiles absorb sound, whereas hard surfaces reflect sound
- wall surfaces: consider material, colour, ease of cleaning and sound absorption
- heating: in-floor heating is preferable to radiators
- ample space in reception/welcome area so parents don't feel rushed
- space for children's outdoor clothing and personal belongings
- storage space for pushchairs and car seats.

(Community Playthings, 2006)

There is considerable practical advice and expertise available to those about to embark on a major building project for the first time. For example, the Sure Start guide *Building for Sure Start: integrated provision for under-fives* is potentially useful for anyone involved in new buildings for the under fives and will have useful material for early years librarians involved in public library projects. The booklet comes in two parts, the client guide and the design guide. The client guide includes a list of questions to ask yourself so that nothing is forgotten in the process of setting up new provision. Another best practice guide aimed at the client is *Creating Excellent Buildings: a guide for clients*. This is divided into the four main stages of a building project – preparation, design, construction and use of the building. The guide provides detailed advice on topics such as:

- establishing the project vision, developing an outline brief and involving stakeholders in the process
- building the in-house client team, establishing roles and responsibilities, and managing the organizational change involved in a building project
- choosing a site or a building for your project
- choosing the most appropriate procurement route
- how to select the architects and consultant team to deliver your project
- developing the detailed design brief for your design team
- the client's role during the construction process
- preparing to use and launching your new building.

Another way to support your decision making is to see what is available elsewhere. You can get ideas for design and use of space by looking at what has already been built. One freely available internet resource is the 'Designing Libraries: the gateway to better library buildings' website. This resource aims to share best practice in the planning and design of library buildings through access to information and images. It includes:

- a database of descriptions and images of recently completed, and in progress, UK and worldwide public library building projects
- a resource for interactively sharing expertise and experience on library planning and design, through discussion forums and e-mail lists
- links to a range of on and offline resources useful to anyone involved in planning, designing or building libraries.

A number of examples from the database are in Sure Start partnerships such as Britwell Play and Learn Library in Slough and Lowestoft Library, which is a shared building. Also included are the Toy Library in Handsworth Library, Birmingham and Platt Bridge Community First School, a new extended school which includes a Sure Start children's centre and nursery provision (**www.designinglibraries.org.uk**).

Early years librarians may not have the loudest voice when it comes to making decisions about the design of the building, but your professional knowledge and expertise can have a very positive impact on the planning discussions. Make sure your professional voice is heard. You should ensure that you are consulted about the needs assessment and to determine specific space requirements.

Case study

Pinmoor Children's Centre

This is the story of a planning project – the design of Bookworms Library at the Pinmoor Children's Centre in Wakefield. It has a beginning, a middle and a successful outcome.

Beginning

Bookworms Library was to form part of the new children's centre at Pinmoor Primary School. The initial design meetings concluded that much of the original design needed altering, particularly the foundation stage unit. Eventually the final plans were completed, accepted by Sure Start then submitted to the local authority for planning permission.

Budget

The final costings came back £200,000 over budget. We were therefore offered the choice of making the development smaller or looking at a modular build. It was advised that a modular build would be cheaper, well within budget and just as good.

Modular build

After visiting other modular builds, it was agreed this approach would be acceptable. Revised plans were drawn up based on the modular design approach. However, budget constraints meant that we had to go back to the original plans, and by this time the project was 8 months behind schedule.

Final plans

The original plans were reviewed and the architects made changes in the costings, which included cutting a large chunk off the library floor area. However, we revised the plans again and by cutting back on the size of the office managed to recoup quite a lot of the space. These plans were accepted, the budget was agreed, and an amendment was made for planning permission. In September 2006 building work eventually started on the new children's centre.

Feelings

It has been a roller-coaster ride of emotions throughout the project. There was excitement at the prospect of having a new children's centre and a brand new purpose-built library. There were also many frustrations as we encountered problems along the way and I came out of some meetings feeling as if little progress was being made. At times it seemed as if it was never going to happen.

The opening

Pinmoor Children's Centre Library opened in October 2007 and was named Bookworms Library by local families. It already forms an important and indispensable part of the local community.

Carol Wootton, Early Years Librarian

Room planning – some things to consider

Remember that a collaborative process encourages people to think about how they are currently doing things and how they would really like to be doing them in the future. You can plan the use of new space, but keep in mind that the fixed features of a building can constrain its interior design. Community Playthings (2006) provides a quick, step-by-step guide to room planning for early years settings. Where possible, build-ins should be kept to a minimum to allow greater flexibility. Try to keep to two doors per room, as a room with too many doors will lose valuable corners and floor space for quiet activities. To free the corners for activity areas, any door should ideally be in the centre of a wall. Try to avoid built-in partitions and shelving, as this will make for less flexible space. In the planning stage also consider electrical outlets, plumbing, floor surface, lighting, and the all-important natural light from windows.

The shape of the room is also important. Bishop and Rimes (2006) argue that many architects underestimate the design challenge of early years. These include the distinctive educational and organizational requirements of the Foundation Stage of the National Curriculum; the importance of the whole environment – indoors and outdoors – for experiential, interactive learning; the Special Educational Needs (SEN) and Disability Act 2001; and the need to integrate education, childcare, family support, adult training, health and other services in children's settings. There is an architectural trend away from rectangular rooms, but Bishop and Rimes feel that, unless the new shape gives children more playing space, it can be detrimental. You need to make up your own mind on this. The Airedale Library and Family Centre in Castleford incorporates a curved wall made of glass bricks as part of the children's centre. The staff feel that this is a positive feature and use it as a display space.

Design to create boundaries

Boundaries increase children's security and focus, protecting their activities from traffic and other distractions, and encouraging longer-lasting, sustained play. You need to think about different uses in the space available and design in quiet corners for reading and noisy stimulating space for role play and group activities. Even in a small room, you can create well defined activity areas, and children will show a higher degree of exploratory behaviour and social interaction. Display and shelving space can act as boundaries and a carpet can be a visual boundary when used to designate the reading corner. Children will instinctively recognize the most secure space in a room. Often the corner directly opposite the entrance is a good place for a quiet area where children can crawl into a cubbyhole or reading hideaway for a bit of privacy. You will also want space for puppet shows and storytelling.

Design to create interactive spaces

Children's facilities are often designed to attract children with playful concepts. The issue desk at the Rainbow Library in Wakefield was designed to look like a farmyard hay cart, and murals in other parts of the library show countryside scenes. The architects BCA designed the younger children's library in New Lenox Public Library in the USA around a 'reading tree' that provides a fun place for parents to share a book with their children. Making dens and dressing up is an integral part of children's play and role play areas allow children to try out well known and new roles in a safe environment.

Flexibility is important and there are advantages in being able to offer a variety of room layouts. This allows for seasonal changes and for catering for different groups with differing needs. New staff members will have different preferences, and space that may be shared by a number of partner organization, needs to be flexible. You can use portable screens and dividers to create small, cosy, safe places for individual work or expand an area for a storytelling group gathering.

Case study

Generating ideas for exciting interactive space

'The Trove' in White Plains Public Library, New York, was opened in October 2005. It is a children's space re-modelled from the old space. The director, Sandra Miranda, wanted to re-create the library for a new generation that is used to being entertained, engaged and active. She looked at museums, playgrounds and bookstores for ideas.

From the outside, the building, which opened in 1974, is a late modernist structure. It wasn't designed from off-the-shelf solutions, and planning the project took several years. The library staff decided what they wanted for the children and worked with a team of other professionals – architects, theatrical designers and fabricators and lighting specialists – to produce the desired end results. The Trove provides different environments and experiences for children from birth through to grade 6. The name was suggested by a branding firm, based on the idea that 'A trove is a collection of valuable items discovered or found'. White Plains Library has created a multisensory, multimedia space. You actually enter The Trove through a jagged brick opening in the wall on the library's second floor – a motif for the traditional library blown apart! The Compass is the focal point of the Trove and serves a number of purposes – information, reference, assistance with circulation and printing.

Each of the environments is very different. The areas closest to the opening are for older children, while areas for younger children are deeper inside The Trove, where it is more contained and intimate.

See further information at http://thetrove.org.

Book display

Choosing books together is an important activity for parents and their babies and young children. As practitioners, we may take our workplace setting for granted, but it is vital to make book selection an enjoyable experience (as illustrated in Figure 3.1). Whitehead (2007) provides observations on the setting, believing that careful thought and organization must go into the environment in which children hear stories and investigate books. Although Whitehead is primarily writing about the early years classroom setting, her ideas are applicable to library environments for very young children. She suggests that the books should be displayed on tables and low shelves, with their attractive covers showing or open at interesting illustrations. A large, unsorted collection of books can be overwhelming and very unappealing and it is suggested that an early years collection should be small and changed frequently (Whitehead, 2007). Versatile, low shelving will allow books to be displayed at child's eye level. Book displays for older children and adults, will use spine-on display to maximize storage, but it is not easy for small children to take books from a tightly packed shelf. Young children and babies will be able to choose their own books when the front pages are facing forward. The storage and display of picture books in mobile kinder boxes also allows for easy browsing by children and their parents. Some manufacturers produce a babies' toy box that can also hold

Figure 3.1 Reading together in the early years

books, so that children can see their toys and books in the clear plastic compartments and can choose what they want to play with.

The Opening the Book company produces a range of play furniture that can double for book display. Its Reading Tower has an upper level with back shelving for older children and a lower level with picture-book shelving for younger children. The sides have metal panels to encourage magnetic games. Another book display idea is the reading tunnel. This piece of library furniture is designed so that young children can have fun crawling through and playing around the tunnel, enjoying physical activity whilst choosing books. Some children's centres support literacy by displaying books that relate to what is going on in the various activity areas rather than just in the more traditional book corner.

Furniture and equipment

Do shop around to get ideas and look at what others are doing. Durability is important, but also consider style and colour combinations. You will have to make a choice within your budget range, but don't feel you have to settle for what is the cheapest. Furniture for the early years library setting should be child-size and sturdy enough to withstand energetic use. It will receive much greater wear and tear than in the average home. From a safety point of view, make sure that edges are rounded to avoid injuries. When choosing furniture it is important not to stick simply to bright primary colours to 'stimulate' children. As will be discussed in more detail later in this chapter, these can have the undesired effect of making some children hyperactive. Consider the types of materials available and the impact they will have on the feel of your library setting. Community Playthings (2006) reminds us that plastic gives an artificial impression; as wood is natural and friendly to the touch, its varieties of pattern and colour provide opportunities for learning.

  It is important to provide an inviting space, enhanced by carpeted floors and toddler-safe furniture. The exposure to language and literature begins with books and reading, so you need spaces where children and the adults looking after them can spend time with books. Comfort is an important consideration. Think carefully about the seating provided for adults, as not everyone wants to relax on floor cushions, however inviting they may appear! Comfortable sofas and rockers are perfect for bonding with babies. You also need some chairs that are low, yet scaled to fit adults, so parents and staff can interact at child level. When considering the purchase of furniture such as tables and chairs ask your suppliers to let you try out before you decide to buy. You can involve parents in helping to choose:

- comfy, squashy sofas
- chairs for daddy bear, mummy bear and baby bear
- contemporary and imaginative seating
- a book loft.

A book loft, or raised area, can be an asset in a children's setting. This can be used to help develop children's imaginative play and is a great place to curl up with a book. If free of detail, it can be used for open-ended play, with the children's imagination rather than prescribed adult ideas determining the scope of play.

  There is a range of companies who supply furniture for the children's library market. Bunnett and Kroll (2006) have described how one early years setting used a variety of different sitting arrangements, using benches, stools and chairs of different heights. With these additional options, they provided interesting physical movement challenges for the children and the space felt more home like.

You can suggest that parents can improvise and create a book den. This is any inviting, fun place for older children to read in. While a comfy chair will often do, a large cardboard box with cut-out windows and door makes a great reading den or cave. Just add a few cushions for comfort. A reading tent is also a great place for creative play and can be quickly made by draping a sheet or a blanket over a table or a clothes horse. A woodland or jungle effect can be created by using large house plants. What better place to read animal and nature stories together?

Carpets and soft furnishings

In baby and toddler spaces in the library the focus is on the floor and it should be soft, warm and draught free. Carpet is one of the best ways of ensuring there is softness in a room and to make it comfortable for small children to sit on the floor. Carpeting is also good for babies, who will spend much of their time on the floor learning to sit, crawl and walk. Carpets can act as a room divider, showing where a story time or group activity area starts. You can use a rug or carpet to help create a reading corner. Some libraries have a brightly coloured alphabet rug to encourage number and letter recognition. This doesn't have to be permanently installed, but can be a large, loose piece with bound edges. This would give you more flexibility in using the available floor space. Floor cushions can be used individually or to settle children down together for a story time session. Ideally, these should be washable! There is a range of fun floor cushions such as:

- Gresswell's Anaconda giant snake
- Loch Ness monster as seen at Pinmoor Children's Centre Library
- story cushions, used very imaginatively in the Seven Stories Artist's Attic (**www.sevenstories.org.uk**), to encourage activities.

Signage and guiding

The signs in your library are an important part of the communication system with users. Signs with friendly wording (in more than one language) will make people feel more welcome. Dewe (2006, 27) discusses how to improve the appeal and signage of library buildings by adopting the ethos of the bookstore, supermarket and other retail outlets. Libraries rely on signs to help users find their way around. Library signs and guiding may be overlooked at the planning stage. Consider the impact on your users and avoid having too many signs and signs with too many words or which are too big or too small. Dewe suggests that signs and guiding perform three main tasks:

- to inform – plans, opening-time notices, safety procedures
- to direct – arrows to destinations
- to identify – when a destination has been reached such as toilets, information desk, baby-changing facilities.

As Olds (2001, 246) advises, the presence of signs clearly denotes an institution, so the fewer the signs the more residential and intimate the setting. The design of signs should be part of the entire interior plan, not an afterthought. Where possible and appropriate, make signs visible to children as well as adults. Child-level devices are desirable – objects to spin, buttons to push, a sequence of photographs of children or animals all help to welcome young ones. Children can interpret signs which use logos or symbols, for example, a crawling baby or the outline of a boy or girl. Signage giving children visual and textual pointers to what is available should be a strong design feature. Makaton signage (a language programme that uses signs and symbols to teach communication, language and literacy skills) can also be displayed and so provide children and families with special educational needs (SEN) full access to resources. Leeds Library and Information Services provides access to Boardmaker software to enable staff and users to make simple signs.

Storage

Storage needs to be considered in the early planning stages for the early years library. Storage should be safe, located close to the point of use and aesthetically pleasing. You can make some storage facilities accessible to children, as they can gain a sense of accomplishment from helping to pack up after a rhyme time or playtime session. Shelves or storage compartments need to be within reach and clearly labelled with simple pictures. This would be good for musical instruments or song sheets. Obviously in a library setting, some storage space will need to be out of the children's reach and may be better behind the scenes in a store cupboard. Here are some examples:

1   A caterpillar hanging bag rack is ideal for storing story sacks.
2   In Wakefield, Carol Wootton used the cellar area in an office building to store the book boxes used for outreach work at a variety of settings. She needed to use her car to get to the various locations and these plastic storage boxes were clipped onto wheels for ease of transport from the cellar to her car boot.
3   The Wensley Fold Children's Centre Library in Blackburn with Darwen operates very successfully from what is, in effect, a large cupboard (as illustrated in Figure 3.2 on the next page). The Literacy Development Officer, Shelley Bullas, explains that this was the best use of the limited space available. The library computer, issue desk and back-up bookstock are kept behind the scenes using sliding doors and are opened up when the library is staffed. At other times the books and resources are on display in the centre and are easily accessible to children and their families.

Stimulation, mood and sound

Children's growth, development and learning are directly affected by the amount of stimulation in their lives. King (2007) writes about the effect of sound and colour on young children. With their still-developing senses of sight, hearing and feeling, they are super-sensitive. We may be unwittingly over-stimulating them with bright primary colours, hard surfaces, loud music

Figure 3.2 Creative use of limited space at Wensley Fold Children's Centre

and bright lights. It is interesting to note that the aforementioned Reggio settings in northern Italy are not painted in bright primary colours. (Community Playthings, 2006, 18). You may actually want to create quiet areas in the library setting by using calming, neutral colours. There are times when you want children to become enthusiastic and involved, but you don't want to over-stimulate.

Colour

We respond to colour with our whole body and colour is often unintentionally the cause of over-stimulation. Nursery-age children are especially responsive to colour. They prefer bright, warm colours, but just because they are so sensitive, surrounding them with lots of primary colour can be over-stimulating. King suggests that hyperactivity, stress, inability to concentrate and even aggressive behaviour can result. Changing the interior colour scheme is one of the easiest and least expensive ways to transform a children's setting. Olds (2001, 213) explains that colour can alter the apparent size and warmth of a room; influence our perception of volume, weight, time, temperature and noise; encourage introversion or extroversion; induce anger or peacefulness. As a form of energy, colour affects our physiology as well as our minds and emotions.

Noise

When designing a library, the impact of 'noise' is an important aspect to consider but it is often overlooked. In a shared public library building there may be some tensions when adult and children's services share space. The adults tend to find the noise from children's library settings intrusive and undesirable, especially when sound from children's activities spills over into 'adult' (quiet) areas of the library. In everyday life both adults and children are constantly pounded with noise. However, unlike adults, who have learned to 'tune out' unwanted noise, children are particularly sensitive to auditory stimulation. Their response is often hyperactivity and irritability. It is important, therefore, to consider how you can damp undesirable noise by using:

- curtains, textured wall hangings and carpets
- furniture, lofts and platforms of varying heights
- sound-absorbent ceiling materials.

Because children and the furniture they use are close to ground level, noise can travel relatively unhindered in the space above their heads. To give a room a more intimate atmosphere, its reverberant qualities can be reduced by adding absorbent surfaces and by varying ceiling and furniture heights. The installation of sound proofing to improve acoustic quality may be considered at the design stage, though this will inevitably have cost implications.

Refreshing spaces – making a tired space into something better

Consider and identify what is working well in your existing space – this could involve staff and user consultation. Prioritize the areas that need the most attention. Clearing out and decluttering can be a good place to start. Does your children's library have a collection development policy that includes guidance on weeding material? You can do practical things like putting wheels on your furniture so you can create a flexible space. Consider what materials or areas in your library currently detract from the environment. If your library has overcrowded shelves, open rubbish bins, scruffy noticeboards and tired-looking signage you can take steps to improve things. It is also a good idea to plan for the future, as styles will change and things will get worn out. A positive approach will involve staff in creating a long-range plan for keeping furnishings and fittings fresh and up to date. This will involve regular cleaning and a replacement policy.

This chapter has considered the physical environment in which the early years library services are provided. In Chapter 4 we will discuss the collection and management of the books and other resources.

Issues and questions

- Consider your role in planning and negotiating the use of space with other professionals.
- Do you take account of how the children naturally use the space in your library?
- What changes do you feel confident to implement now you have read this chapter?

Key points to remember

- There are many useful sources of guidance available.
- Thinking about user needs is important – think creatively and enjoy the process.
- Never miss a planning meeting (if you can help it) – your role includes the skills of planning, design and negotiation.
- Don't underestimate your practitioner knowledge.

Useful organizations

Blackburn with Darwen Borough, **www.blackburn.gov.uk**
CABE: the Commission for Architecture and the Built Environment,
    www.cabe.org.uk
Community Playthings, **www.communityplaythings.co.uk**
Froebel Educational Institute, **www.froebel.org.uk**
Opening the Book, **www.openingthebook.com**
Steiner Waldorf, **www.steinerwaldorf.org/earlyyears.html**

4

Resources for early years libraries – books, toys and other delights

Introduction

This chapter is about the most important resources in the early years library - those are, of course, the books with their exciting stories, tantalizing tales and wonderful pictures and illustrations. However, this chapter is not just about collections of books but also about how to select and collect a range of resources to meet community needs, in particular the target audience of young children and their families. A range of exciting resources should be available in the bright, welcoming environment of the early years library (as illustrated in Figure 4.1 on the next page). It is important to have knowledge about children and their families' culture, heritage, language and interests, so as to ensure that a breadth of valuable resources is provided. The chapter also illustrates why early years librarians need to have knowledge of diverse resources such as treasure baskets, toy libraries, story sacks and Bookstart packs. We will discuss how to select books that are appropriate for babies and young children, girls and boys, additional-language learners and children with special educational needs, not forgetting their parents. Sources of information to facilitate selection, and reviews of resources, have been included to make this job easier.

Collection development and management

Before we take a more detailed look at the resources in an early years collection, consider the underlying principles and requirements of collection

Figure 4.1 A wide range of resources in a bright and welcoming environment

development. An understanding of this is important if you are to be an effective advocate for your library and user community. To be able to manage your resources effectively it is good practice to have an understanding of how your organization operates and knowledge of the local policies. The starting point in collection development is to decide what stock (resources and materials) you are going to include in the library. How is this decided?

Information and guidance should be available in the documents produced by library authorities. Many libraries will create collection development policies and stock selection guides to better plan their collections and to justify the allocation of resources. This documentation should reflect statutory requirements and legislation and the requirement to provide resources within a best-value framework. Libraries are under scrutiny to get better value for money from the suppliers who provide books and other resources. Although library authorities will have different approaches to how this is managed, the underlying principles are the same. Collection development is defined as:

The process of planning a library's stock acquisitions first to cater for immediate needs, and more importantly to acquire a collection capable of meeting future requirements. The term implies a desire for a depth and quality of stock, but it cannot be separated from the need to exploit the collection effectively.

(Feather and Sturgess, 1997, 61)

As a management principle, stock should be selected on the basis of written guidelines and criteria to ensure that there will be a unified approach and that the selection methodology will be cost effective. Some key questions to be considered are:

- how stock is selected and made accessible
- how stock is maintained and promoted
- why some stock is kept and other material is removed.

The stock policy or collection management plan will provide an overall statement relating to the acquisition, selection and withdrawal of stock for the organization. It should be kept under regular review and seen as an evolving document, to reflect the needs of the community it serves. Communities change over time and data can be gathered to aid decision making through community profiling (as discussed in Chapter 2).

Library authorities can take a number of different approaches to the procurement and supply of books and other resources. One option is to outsource key traditional functions like book selection, cataloguing and acquisitions. Libraries deciding to outsource will go 'out to tender' to select the best-value supplier for the procurement process. This 'supplier selection' means that all general library materials are selected by the supplier, usually based on a set of requirements provided by the library customer. It is recognized that very specific requirements, for example, Asian-language materials, may need to be purchased from specialist suppliers and publishers outside of the contract. An argument in favour of using the supplier-selection approach is that time saved as a result can be used to deliver front-line services. Leeds Library and Information Services uses supplier selection to acquire stock for the 55 libraries and network of mobile libraries across the metropolitan area. A detailed specification is provided to the book supplier, which includes a stock spending plan for the early years category. This is regularly updated and staff can add titles to the lists. A number of library authorities also gain benefits through consortium membership, where bulk purchasing arrangements aim to reduce costs while improving efficiencies in terms of supply times and availability of materials.

In contrast to the supplier-selection model, many library services still work independently by procuring stock directly from suppliers on an individual basis. Some public library authorities have established buying teams to select children's stock. Staff will use various methods to select resources, by looking at books themselves in selection meetings or in suppliers' show-rooms and by using publishers' lists, catalogues and trade publications. Many staff may be involved in the selection and some authorities will ask for feedback from readers. There are pros and cons in the different approaches to procurement, based on financial and other criteria. Effective practitioners will be familiar with the procedures in their organization.

The plan may also include:

- guidelines for collection maintenance, as worn-out stock will need to be withdrawn – this activity is often referred to as weeding the collection
- guidelines for in-service training of current and future staff.

The situation with regard to supply of library stock may not be so clear in some children's centres, as it will depend on the funding and partnership arrangements.

The early years collection

Having considered the general principles of how library authorities acquire stock, let us look in more detail at collection development in the early years library. Books will form the core, but remember also that the collection in an early years library 'is a physical entity which includes materials in print and in visual, auditory, tactile and electronic formats with appropriate forms of delivery' (Van Orden and Bishop, 2001, 12). The resources will be expanded to include babies, infants and toddlers and should provide materials in a variety of formats to encourage play, creativity and development – the emphasis is on having fun.

What is the role of the early years librarian in collection development? The librarian's professional skills include the selection and use of materials, and this involves decision-making skills. If we look to a professional library source the IFLA *Guidelines for Children's Library Services* state that:

> Children's libraries should include a variety of developmentally appropriate materials in all formats, including printed materials (books, periodicals, comics, brochures), media (CDs, DVDs, cassettes), toys, learning games, computers, software and connectivity. (2003, 9)

The process of creating the policy for the early years is important, as it will involve a knowledge and understanding of the particular user community. As with any service provider, you need to assess the needs of your market before you can begin to provide the resources. The allocation of limited budgets requires careful and well informed decision making; this is an important aspect of business planning. The planning will identify the community or market to be served, and will describe the product – the materials that are available and how to acquire them. It is important to involve those with a vested interest, for example, you can include parents in developing ideas for the parenting collection, which will be discussed later in this chapter. Sharing information about the collection development plan or stock plan can also be a public relations tool. For the library this can be another means of communicating with the stakeholders. Many libraries publish their collection development and stock plans on the local authority website.

The purpose of the collection development plan in an early years library setting is to establish guidelines for current and future staff on acquiring stock and developing the collection. The plan will create a collection development policy which explains why certain materials are in the collection. It could include the selection criteria and the procedures used, as selection is a complex decision-making process. Selecting materials within a framework of given criteria can be regarded as good practice. It may not be enough to say 'I've done this for years – I just know what is needed in the early years library', or 'I like this particular author', or 'Chris, who runs the library in the community centre makes the decisions'. Some librarians make selections based on guidelines passed on by word of mouth. The feeling may be: why bother documenting what you do in practice as these decisions are based on experience? While not wishing to decry experience or knowledge, in our opinion this informal approach is not very professional from a management perspective. You will leave yourself open to being challenged on the type and quantity of materials you are providing, and in the current financial climate it is more than likely you will have to defend the budget allocations. A policy designed and produced by those who have best knowledge of the library service and its users should make planning easier for the future.

Staff are an important source of information about the collection and how it is used. Librarians have a vested interest in developing language and reading skills. The selection and acquisition policies should ensure the availability of appropriate materials for both children and their parents and carers. The materials should be acquired in a planned, systematic way and should reflect language and cultural backgrounds. Involving parents in selection is a valuable way of building good partnerships with the user community.

How do you do it? Guidelines for book selection

The IFLA *Guidelines for Children's Library Services* (2003, 9) provide the following information on selection criteria:

> Building collections and services, librarians should choose materials which are
>
> - high quality
> - age appropriate
> - current and accurate
> - a reflection of a variety of values and opinions
> - a reflection of local community culture
> - an introduction to the global community.

What information should be included in a collection development document? How do librarians decide what book stock is important to acquire? We can look at examples from Kirklees Cultural Services and the Bookstart programme to get some idea of criteria for selecting the all-important children's books.

Example 1: Children's book selection – Kirklees Cultural Services

- **Board books**
  Sturdy form. Clear photos or pictures, minimum, clear text, bright colours. Can be tactile or have flaps, etc. to stimulate the senses. Content – everyday, familiar objects/situations. Rhythm, rhyme and repetition. Questions and sound effects. Age: suitable for babies and toddlers from birth to two years.
- **Picture books**
  Larger format, longer stories. Language can be more challenging. Content as before but also can be more imaginative, abstract, dealing with the wider world and developing emotions. Pictures carry story as well as text. Age: approximately 2–5yrs.
- **'Learners' for beginner readers**
  Generally one short story. Simple sentences. Smaller format (around 50 pages). Well illustrated – speech bubbles are clear and not too complex. Age: 5–7 years.
- **Parents' collection**
  — Books to support parenting skills and the development of early childhood skills e.g. reading, writing, maths and play. Age range: for parents of children aged 5 years and under.
  — Hand in hand. Picture books and some information books for children that deal with special situations and are better suited for use in conjunction with an adult, e.g.:
    - dealing with change: moving house, new baby, death
    - new experiences: visiting the dentist, flying in an aeroplane.

Branching Out website

Example 2: Book selection for Bookstart

Bookstart is the national agency promoting books and reading to people of every age and culture in the UK. The Bookstart packs are very successful and well known. Wendy Cooling, Bookstart's founder, explains that the books for the packs are selected by an independent panel which includes health visitors, speech and language therapists, early years educationalists and librarians. The varied cultural and social backgrounds of the children must be taken into account so choosing them is not as easy as it might sound.

> People forget that I'm buying books to go into every household in the country. I can't send everyone a very white, middle-class book with mummy, daddy, boy and girl. They'd probably bin it. I wouldn't buy a book totally centred on a pig, because of Muslim families. I worked with one-parent teenage mothers, and the last thing they wanted was a nice 'daddy' book. I'm looking for books that can literally go into any home and not cause offence.   (Cooling, 2007)

As a charity, Bookstart cannot afford to pay standard wholesale prices, so the team negotiates with publishers to buy the books very cheaply. Not all publishers can meet Bookstart's budget, so some titles cannot be included in the scheme. Bookstart provides details of its 'Policy on the selection process and criteria for books for Bookstart' on its website. The following criteria are used for choosing Bookstart pack books and recommending books in Bookstart book lists:

1) Quality of materials
   Books must be well produced and printed. Board books must be safe and sturdy enough for the purpose. All books must meet the stringent health and safety standards of the UK and Europe and have the CE quality mark.

2) Content and suitability
   We use two books that have a good combination of all these qualities in our packs:

   - books that are well illustrated and well photographed, that have appropriate text

- feely-touchy, interactive books that are exciting for babies and toddlers
- books suitable for the age range
- books that reflect baby's/child's experiences
- rhyme, rhythm and repetition, which are fun for babies and children and helps them to learn

We are committed to Equal Opportunities and address race and gender issues.

3) Cost and availability
   We generally purchase books at cost price or below from a range of children's publishers who have offered their help and have said they are 'Proud to Support Bookstart'.

Library collections will be shaped by the needs of the user community. The needs of the community cannot be effectively assessed by relying on data about materials already in demand and being circulated. This is one way of showing the needs and wants of the community but will only relate to the current user base and the materials already in the library stock. You will want to reach out so as to encourage potential users to access your services. Data collected via community profiling can be used to inform decision making about the resources you should provide at local level.

Consider your policies and procedures relating to collection development and the loan and circulation of material to this client group. It is important to encourage parents to borrow the library materials to use in their home environment. This means that you need to consider having multiple copies of popular books and 'easy' joining and borrowing policies and procedures. Many parents can be put off by misconceptions about complicated joining regulations and heavy fines for overdue materials.

Selecting the book stock for an early years collection should be a very enjoyable experience, and Whitehead (2007), an early years specialist, says that choosing books for young children is a great responsibility, as we are directly influencing the views they will develop about literature, books and reading.

Selecting books for the early years collection
Selecting picture books

Picture books are the core of an early years library collection and are important because they enable us to explore the world around us. They will include books with multicultural content and can help to reflect the families in your catchment area as well as a view of the wider world. Children's Laureate Michael Rosen is championing the 'The Big Picture', a Booktrust national campaign promoting picture books. He says that

> Picture books are the fuse that lights our awareness that reading is full of intense pleasures.   (Booktrust, 2007)

Picture books and illustrations encourage children's vocabulary development, as the adult supplies the word or words for pictures. Young children soon become accomplished at matching the words with the pictures. In early stages of language acquisition they will make appropriate sounds, which gradually turn into words over time. Parents soon begin to know whether the sound being uttered is the correct 'word' for each picture, as they will have developed knowledge about their child. Animal pictures are normally a very successful way into early sound and word formation, with cows mooing, lions roaring and dogs barking. Children can communicate meanings through sounds before they can articulate words. They also gain familiarity with objects and concepts, which develops both their vocabulary and their knowledge and understanding of the world. Large picture and storybooks enable children to get physically involved in pointing out what is happening and in labelling the characters and objects. Brock and Rankin give an example of a favourite picture book being shared across the generations: 'every new baby in our family is presented with a copy of the Ahlberg's *The Baby's Catalogue*. The pictures reflect what we do in our family life.' (Brock and Rankin , 2008, 67).

Books that are good for babies and toddlers will have:

- thick, sturdy cover and pages
- small size, for little hands
- bright, colourful pictures

- simple geometric shapes
- clear pictures
- pictures of human faces
- few words
- nursery rhymes.

Selecting board books

Board books with easy-to-see pictures and high contrast between the object and the background are excellent for a baby. Board books are easy for tiny fingers to handle and the pages won't tear. Babies respond best to books that have sharp contrast between the picture and the background. Wordless picture books provide an opportunity to make up stories to go with the pictures and lift-the-flap books add an element of delicious anticipation. For toddlers the story can be more involved and pictures can have more detail. It is good to choose things they can relate to, such as pets or animals, dressing and meal times, and what they see and do as part of everyday life. Stories with rhyme and rhythm are also good, as are stories with repeated phrases or repeated happenings. To be inclusive, try to select books which have good father figures as well as mums.

Selecting dual-language books for the bilingual child

As stated in previous chapters, librarians should have knowledge about their client group, about the diversity of the communities and families. This should include knowledge of and respect for their different cultures, heritage and languages.

> In government documentation, the term most commonly used for children who speak other languages beside English is EAL (English as an additional language) learners . . . we use the term 'bilingual because we believe it is broader and more inclusive, and represents more accurately the important idea, that for bilingual children, all their languages contribute to their whole language experience and their knowledge of the world.
>
> (Conteh and Brock, 2006, 2-3)

Through books, stories and illustrations, bilingual children can be introduced to new and complex language, contextualized in meaningful and interesting experiences. Story is thus an effective vehicle for shaping language in powerful and exciting ways (Conteh and Brock, 2006). Language and culture are central to identity, personal, social and emotional development, and it is therefore very important to reflect children's linguistic diversity and cultural heritage in the books they look at and have read to them. Parents also need to feel that they are involved in the learning processes and so need to have access to books that reflect their own cultural heritage, with stories and information that can help them to expand their children's experiences and knowledge. Parents in Bradford's Earlystart Project valued the books that had dual-language texts in their own first language and in English. They also appreciated that their children's first language and their burgeoning bilingualism was valued and respected by practitioners.

> I particularly like borrowing dual language books because my husband can't speak English but can read to our child in Bengali, which makes him feel involved. (Brock and Power, 2006, 23)

There are now quite a number of books that have been translated into dual-language texts – including the 'Where's Spot' series, *Dear Zoo* and *Mitthu the Parrot*, to mention only a few, which are in languages as diverse as Vietnamese, Gujarati, Chinese and Urdu. There are valuable organizations and websites noted at the end of this chapter to guide you to lists of books and stories that are ideal to use when working with bilingual children. The International Digital Children's Library provides free internet access to children's books in their original languages and this resource is discussed in more detail later in this chapter.

Selecting books for young boys

It is important to dispel the myth that boys do not like books. On the contrary, find a topic that engages a boy's interest, and he can easily be engrossed in a book. Favourites are topics such as pirates, castles, adventures, exploring or stories about boys and their fathers. Figure 4.2 illustrates boys enjoying time in the library.

Figure 4.2 Boys enjoying time in the library

Scenario: Josh and Andrew as library users

Josh, aged 5, and Andrew, aged 3, now visit their local library regularly. Their parents had explained to the boys that the library was a place to be quiet and they behaved very well. On the first visit they stayed three hours; the boys were engrossed. Simon, their dad, brought them on their third visit and was amazed how calm and absorbed they were.

Josh loves information books, particularly transport – cars, ships, rockets and anything about dinosaurs and animals. At home his mum is reading him Roald Dahl books, serialising *The BFG*, *The Enormous Crocodile* and *Fantastic Mr Fox*. During one library visit Josh found the tapes and CDs and brought them to show his mum; she had not realized they could be borrowed and the boys are now listening to story tapes in the car.

Scenario: Young Tom the pirate

Four-year-old Tom loves pirates – he has been known to dress up as a pirate, complete with eye-patch, hat and even temporary tattoos. He has a pirate playscape and pirate finger puppets. His favourite book is *1001 Pirate Things to Spot* by Usborne.

Selecting books for children with special educational needs

Research on the Bookstart project has clearly shown that giving babies a love of books from the earliest age makes an enormous difference to language development and listening skills. Stories, songs and rhymes are also important in supporting bonding and developing a sense of well-being. This is no different for young children who are blind or partially sighted or deaf. This section looks at some of the resources developed to support babies and young children who have special educational needs.

Booktouch

Booktouch is a freely available Bookstart pack for blind and partially sighted babies and children aged from birth to four years. Around 800 babies born each year are eligible for a Booktouch pack containing touch-and-feel books, some of which are in Braille. The pack and accompanying guidance leaflet were designed by Booktrust with advice from RNIB and ClearVision (a national postal lending library). All babies need help in learning how a book works, which way to hold it, how to turn the pages and eventually to associate the marks on the page with language. The same is true for blind and partially sighted children, many of whom will eventually be able to read large print. Booktouch helps children become familiar with the concept of gathering information via their fingers. This is important for every child, but particularly for those who will go on to learn to read Braille, and read maps and diagrams by touch.

The pack also includes a leaflet with helpful tips about sharing books. Some of these tips will be the same as for any child - for example, all young children will enjoy it if you make sound effects to go with a story. But there are a few more considerations involved in reading with blind and partially sighted children and advice is given on what kind of pictures are best, what kind of text is easiest to read and what to consider when choosing books. Local authority visual impairment teachers provided advice on the most appropriate books to include in the pack.

ClearVision

ClearVision is a national postal lending library of over 12,000 children's books with the text added in Braille or Moon (a simpler alternative to Braille). ClearVision books are designed for children with little or no sight to share with sighted children and adults. The collection includes tactile board books, simple stories for young children and stimulating books for newly fluent readers. ClearVision books are borrowed by over 800 families, schools, visual impairment services and libraries all over the UK. Anyone in the UK who needs children's books with a Brailled text is welcome to join the ClearVision library. The books are ordinary children's picture books with added Braille (or Moon). They do not have enlarged print and are therefore not especially suitable for partially sighted children learning to read print. The books are designed to be shared and are suitable for any child who is learning Braille or who may do so in the future. Some of their 'readers' are babies and toddlers whose parents are keen to get them used to feeling Braille long before they learn to read it - in the same way as fully sighted babies see print everywhere before they can make sense of it.

ClearVision currently lends books to over 100 public libraries in the UK for an annual membership fee. Libraries can then lend on a local basis, enabling Braille readers to use the local library along with their families or schools. ClearVision also lends books to about 130 families with visually impaired children throughout the UK. Membership is free for families, who are also welcome to contact ClearVision at any time to comment on the books or to request books on specific topics. Further information is available at **www.clearvision.project.org**.

Bookshine

Bookstart has added 'Bookshine' packs to its existing range of materials.

Bookshine will help parents of deaf babies and children discover books together. The books and accompanying guidance materials for parents and carers have been chosen in partnership with the National Deaf Children's Society (NDCS) and parents of deaf children. The pack includes a touch-and-feel book and a book featuring simple British Sign Language (BSL) signs and an image of a child with a hearing aid, as it is important that deaf children see themselves in books.

Selecting books for the parenting collection

Library services will be very focused on promoting exciting materials for young library users, but don't forget the needs of their parents and carers. Most parents are not trained or educated about how to raise children. First-time parents, in particular, may be looking for information on how to bring up the new member of their family. In some cultures, parenting practice may be based on family tradition or experiences. Where such traditional advice may not be available, information may be gained from professional practitioners. Families are also exposed to information and ideas through popular media: there are now many parenting magazines on the newsagents' shelves and 'nanny-says' types of programme on the television about coping with babies and toddlers. Parents who are well informed and feel confident and supported are better able to understand their role and provide good childcare. In communities where there is a lack of support and isolation in the parenting role, the adults risk stress and depression. Libraries can support the information needs of parents and carers by providing a parenting collection of books and other resources and by offering referral services when working in partnership with other organiz-ations and agencies.

Parents need to know that the link between their involvement and the literacy environment of the home leads to a child's success at school. Familiarize yourself with reference materials and electronic sources aimed at parents and other professionals that support the family – this will be helpful in developing your role in the interdisciplinary teamwork supporting the Every Child Matters agenda. One way to provide education and support for parents and carers is to provide a collection of materials specifically aimed to meet their needs. These collections can include books, pamphlets, DVDs and audio books. Some parents may be first encouraged to use a computer in the library setting, and one idea is to bookmark websites on child development and parenting issues so as to promote computer literacy and encourage families to use the facilities. Experience has shown that it can be important to locate the parenting collection where it is easily accessible from the children's area.

> Leeds Libraries and Information Services have a 'family matters' collection in each of the 55 libraries in Leeds. This includes books on family, feelings, health, new experiences, being safe and family learning. The 'healthy living' collections include books and DVDs designed to help families get healthy and stay healthy.

Selection and management of the parenting collection

From a collection management perspective, the selection, acquisition, marketing and eventual weeding or withdrawal of the stock needs to be built into the ongoing work of the early years library. Agreement should be reached on the range of topics to be covered and the scope of the parenting collection. Who decides what goes in this collection? Are there selection criteria? Topics for inclusion are likely to include general parenting, childcare, breastfeeding, toilet training, literacy and reading. There are some other considerations. The parenting collection should reflect the cultural diversity of the community it serves, but this may raise policy issues about the type of material you decide to provide. The parenting collection may be expanded to include material of interest to parents of school-age or teenaged children, as they may be the older siblings of your babies and young children. Some libraries target teen parents, who will have very specific support needs. Another policy decision is whether to provide duplicate copies of parenting resources in the main library collection and in branch and mobile collections.

Other resources in the early years library

In addition to the all-important books, the library can provide a range of exciting resources to encourage the development of language and literacy across the community. In this section we will discuss the provision of storysacks, treasure baskets and toy libraries.

Storysacks and storybags

Originally devised by Neil Griffith, a storysack is a large cloth bag containing a children's book and supporting materials to stimulate reading activities and make shared reading a memorable and enjoyable experience. The sack can contain soft toys of the book's main characters, and props and scenery that parents and other adults can use with children to bring a book to life even if the adult's reading skills are limited. The sack may include a non-fiction book on the same theme, an audio-tape of the story, a language-based game and a short guide containing questions to ask, words to consider and other ways to extend the reading activity. Storysacks are a popular, non-threatening way of encouraging parents and carers to start sharing stories with their children, especially those parents with little positive experience of books.

By encouraging children and adults to enjoy reading together, a storysack gives a child the chance to enjoy books at a variety of levels. Children can:

- develop their listening skills as the stories are read to them
- improve their vocabulary by talking about the contents of the sack
- develop their social skills and improve confidence
- explore different cultures and inclusion issues.

Storysack Ltd offers a wide range of commercially produced storysacks for sale, as well as tips on how to use the sacks. Further details are available from **www.storysack.com**. The company also produce a storysack rack – on castors, with storage space for holding big books. Although storysacks can be bought, another idea behind them is that you can get the community involved in a project to make storysacks or storybags. If you have parents who can sew, then decide on which book you want to make a storybag for and what you want in the bag and ask the parents to design it. By doing this you can get the whole community involved, and also raise their interest in their children's reading. Research evidence suggests that many adults, after they have been involved in a storysacks project, are motivated to take up opportunities for further study and so improve their own skills.

Many libraries manage various storysack projects, aiming to reach people in deprived areas and groups at risk of social exclusion because of their language, culture or abilities. The themes of the sacks may address issues faced by these groups. The libraries work in partnership with community groups and their supporting agencies. Based on the same principle as storysacks, Hampshire County Council has developed a number of storybaskets as part of The Living Album project. These give children an opportunity to learn about Hampshire's Gypsy heritage and the Gypsy and Traveller lifestyles. Two of the baskets are housed in a 'Reading Wagon' storybox, adapted to look like a traditional Gypsy wagon. The storybaskets contain a storybook, a tape recording of the story with a small cassette player, as well as 'smell cubes' and objects which relate to the story. Each of the selected titles not only relates to Gypsies and Travellers but also explores ideas and issues around acceptance, tolerance and inclusion. The storybaskets enable childcare providers to discuss cultural and racial issues in a fun and sensitive way. For further information about The Living Album project see the website at **www.hants.gov.uk/rh/gypsy**.

Babies love treasure baskets

The early years library can expand the range of resources to provide multi-sensory resources. The treasure basket is the perfect educational 'toy' for babies who are not yet able to crawl and is a great exploratory resource as soon as they are able to sit, propped up with cushions. The treasure basket itself is a basket made from a natural material such as wicker. It is filled with natural and inexpensive everyday objects from the real world and found around the home (as illustrated in Figure 4.3 on the next page). They provide babies with sensory stimulation and help to develop hand-eye co-ordination, making choices and preferences. The concept was developed over 30 years ago by Elinor Goldshmied, a child psychologist, from observing children and the way they gained knowledge of the world around them. She developed a method of play that helps babies and toddlers to learn naturally. 'Heuristic play' is the term used to describe play for babies and

Figure 4.3 Creating a treasure basket

infants that actively encourages exploration of natural objects by using and developing their senses (Goldschmied and Jackson, 2004).

A treasure basket is full of interesting objects that babies want to investigate and that they can play with, with little or no adult help. Often they will get very excited and will smile and clap, making 'happy' noises. By sucking, mouthing and handling objects, babies are finding out about size, shapes, smell, sound and texture. Goldschmied suggests that none of the objects in a treasure basket should be a 'bought toy' or made of plastic. In the highly manufactured 'global north' babies are already surrounded by plastic objects which are smooth, have no smell and no taste. By offering a range of objects which are not plastic you can increase the opportunities for a baby to learn and explore. In this age of consumerism, you can also help parents to understand that there are alternatives to brightly coloured and often expensive plastic toys.

The contents should be selected with safety in mind, they require regular care and maintenance and should be washable, wipeable or disposable. They should be small enough to be held by tiny hands but large enough not to be swallowed. Table 4.1 on the next page gives examples of items you can include in a treasure basket.

You can also try using a themed approach by devising a 'touch wood' basket, the 'bathroom basket' or the 'brush basket'. Another idea is to create a 'sounds' treasure basket filled with different musical instruments and sound makers.

Toy libraries

The constructive use of toys can help a child's development. Community toy libraries were first formed in England in the late 1960s, initially for children with additional needs. A report from the National Association of Toy and Leisure Libraries (2007) looks at the contribution that toy libraries make in securing better outcomes for children and the support they offer to parents and the wider community. Today there are an estimated 1000 toy libraries serving a quarter of a million children and their families. The study drew on five case studies operating in areas of economic and social disadvantage in different parts of England. The report urges that consideration be given to including a toy library in every children's centre and within extended schools provision. Toy libraries can engage parents who otherwise might not use early years play services.

When choosing new stock you will need to strike a balance between toys that are widely available and the more specialist items. Toy library toys have to be really sturdy, very safe, and cleanable. They also need to appeal to both boys and girls and to represent all sections of the community. Greene (1991, 49) has suggested the following criteria for choosing toys:

- safety
- durability
- child appeal or play value

- aesthetic value – should be well designed
- teaching and learning potential.

Table 4.1 Examples of items that can be included in a treasure basket

Natural objects	Objects in leather, textile, rubber, fur
Fir cones	Puppy 'bone'
Large pebbles	Leather purse
Shells	Coloured marble 'eggs'
Large chestnuts	Velvet powder puff
Big feathers	Fur ball
Pumice stone	Length of rubber tubing
Large corks	Tennis ball
Small natural sponge	Golf ball
A lemon	Small teddy bear
An apple	Bean bag
	Small cloth bags containing lavender, rosemary, thyme, cloves
Wooden objects	**Metal objects**
Small boxes, velvet lined	Spoons – various sizes
Rattles	Small egg whisk
Bamboo whistle	Bunch of keys
Castanets	Lemon squeezer
Clothes pegs	Garlic squeezer
Cylinders – bobbin, cotton reel	Bottle brush
Napkin ring	Triangle
Spoon	Metal egg cup
Egg cup	Tea strainer
Objects of natural materials	**Paper, cardboard, etc.**
Woollen ball	Little notebook with spiral rings
Little baskets	Greaseproof paper
Small raffia mat	Tinfoil
Wooden nailbrush	Small cardboard boxes
Toothbrush	Insides of kitchen-paper rolls
Shaving brush	
House-painting brush	
Source: Based on Goldschmied and Jackson (2004, 108–10)	

As outlined above, safety is a major consideration when choosing toys for the library, so it is important to ensure that the products are well made, with no sharp or protruding parts that could injure the children. They need to be free from toxic substances such as lead, not easily broken, yet easy to keep clean. A further consideration is the need to match the toys to the stages of development and emerging abilities of young children. This is not only to enhance their ability to learn but also to increase their enjoyment of playing with the toy.

Toys for babies and young infants

Babies like nothing better than to reach out for objects and place them in their mouths. There are many books for babies that can be chewed and wiped clean, like board books, bath books and flannel books and these are ideal for babies and infants. It is therefore good to have on hand toys that babies can handle and suck, such as large rings, teething toys and squeeze toys. They like things that they can shake and that make a noise, so rattles of all designs are good, as well as objects with interesting textures, such as textured balls, vinyl and board books. All these toys can be good for developing listening skills, concentration, hand–eye co-ordination and gross and fine motor skills. As babies grow a little older, they love to move around and explore the environment. Toys that encourage movement, such as plastic and wooden vehicles with wheels that they can either ride or push along by themselves are good for the development of gross motor skills and concentration.

Toys for toddlers and young children

Toddlers are rapidly learning language. Good toys are things to play 'pretend' with, such as child-size furniture – kitchen sets with kitchen appliances, chairs and play food – or baby dolls and their accessories, like doll beds, prams and push-chairs. Dressing-up accessories and toy phones are also ideal for encouraging language acquisition, as are puppets, stuffed toys, plastic animals, sand and water toys. Young children love running around, jumping, climbing, rolling, and rough-and-tumble play. It is therefore good to provide toys which encourage the use of their large and small muscles, such as balls for kicking and throwing, ride-on equipment, low climbers with soft material underneath, as well as toys for pounding on and hammering. They also enjoy problem-solving toys – so be sure to provide wooden puzzles, construction kits, blocks that snap together, objects to sort, as well as things with hooks, buttons, buckles, and snaps, or toys with parts that do things, such as dials, switches, knobs, lids and zips.

Children learn through play, and toys are their tools. The following suggestion from Family Place Libraries is a sample of age-appropriate toys available for very young children:

- infant non-shatter mirror
- small bead toy
- nesting cups
- shape sorter
- foam, cardboard or vinyl blocks
- cause and effect toy (with lids that are easily opened by manipulating various switches)
- knobbed puzzles
- Lego
- puppets
- small kitchen set (plates, cups, etc.)
- foldable train mat with magnetic train cars
- animal figures (farm, jungle).

Selecting videos and DVDs

Age-appropriate videos and DVDs can provide an excellent source of entertainment and be a valuable educational resource for young children. They provide visual and verbal stimuli and can be good for developing communication and extending vocabulary.

Selecting audio tapes and CDs

Tapes and CDs of stories are good reading partners, as they allow the child to listen to a favourite story over and over again. They are also great for journeys in the car. In the Rankin family many long car journeys to holiday destinations were made bearable by listening to Roald Dahl stories. Dad particularly enjoyed *Danny the Champion of the World* and we all were word perfect on *The Enormous Crocodile*. Listening to a story tape also allows children to match spoken sounds to words on the page.

Music resources – opportunities for listening and participation

The Early Years Foundation Stage (DfES, 2007) state that you need to promote opportunities for children to:

- share and enjoy a wide range of rhymes, music, songs
- link language with physical movement in action songs and rhymes
- develop phonological awareness through small-group and individual teaching.

Recent research on the impact of musical activities on the development of pre-school children shows that regular contact with musicians has a positive impact on the development of communication skills and social, physical and cultural development (Music Manifesto, 2006). Consider the resources needed for music making and where to obtain them. Suggested items are rhythm instruments and keyboards, xylophones, maracas and tambourines.

Computer programs for young children

Computer programs that are interactive (the child can do something) and that children can understand (the software uses graphics and spoken instruction, not just print), and where children can control the software's pace and path provide children with opportunities to explore a variety of concepts on several levels.

Sources of information for early years stock selection

There are many sources of information you can use to support the process of selecting stock. Specialist journals and reader-development magazines are a good starting point.

Books for Keeps

This is a bi-monthly children's books review magazine. It often has a themed focus for each issue. The reviews are organized into teaching ranges. There are feature articles about different aspects of children's books, including production and promotion. The print version is available on subscription; the online version provides free access to reviews of thousands of children's books.

URL: **www.booksforkeeps.co.uk**.

Carousel – the guide to children's books

This is the magazine of the Federation of Children's Book Groups. Available via subscription and published three times a year, it is a well illustrated publication with articles on children's literature and publishing and author interviews. It also includes book reviews - fiction and non-fiction - and reviews of audio books.

Carousel, The Saturn Centre, 54-76 Bissell Street, Birmingham B5 7HX
URL: **www.carouselguide.co.uk**

Achuka

This is an online magazine showcasing the world of children's books.

URL: **www.achuka.co.uk**

There are also a number of non-specialist sources which are worth checking. Special features and book reviews appear in, for example, *The Bookseller*, *The Guardian*, *The Sunday Times*, *Times Educational Supplement* and *The Observer*.

Book sources

Booktrust *Best Book Guide*

Booktrust publishes a free guide to its selected best books for ages 5 and under. The *Best Book Guide* reviews can be downloaded from the website or requested in print format.

URL: **www.booktrustchildrensbooks.org.uk/Recommended-Books**

Centre for Literacy in Primary Education
Simply the best books for children: books for 0–7 years
   URL: **www.clpe.co.uk**

School Library Association
Riveting Reads: 3–6 by Derek Jowett (2005)
   This list of more than 250 books is arranged under a variety of
   headings, such as Starting Out and Families. They have been
   chosen with parents, library staff and teachers in mind and can be
   used at home as well as by teachers working in nursery schools,
   pre-school groups and at Key Stage 1.
   URL: **www.sla.org.uk/riveting-reads.php**

The Ultimate Book Guide (2008)
   This is a National Year of Reading guide aimed at new library
   members. It includes *The Ultimate First Book Guide* sections on
   recommended titles for early years covering 0–2 years and 2–5 years.
   URL: **www.ultimatebookguide.com**

The Ultimate First Book Guide: over 500 great books for 0–7 year olds by Leonie
Flynn and Daniel Hahn, A&C Black (2008)
   The guide covers board books and novelty books, through to classic
   and contemporary picture books, chapter books and more
   challenging reads.

Publishers and booksellers

The websites of publishers and booksellers are a useful source of information
on new titles. Bookshops specializing in children's books.
   URL: **www.booktrusted.co.uk/information/bookshops.php4**

Internet based resources
Booktrust

This is an independent national charity 'that encourages people of all ages and cultures to discover and enjoy reading'. The website provides free resources and recommendations for librarians, teachers and parents about books for all ages. Users can search the website for recommended books using keywords, genre and age range. Information is also provided on specialist children's bookshops, specialist children's literature magazines, publishers and organizations working with children's books and the children's literacy sector.

URL: **www.booktrusted.co.uk/books**

International Digital Children's Library – a library for the world's children

The International Digital Children's Library (ICDL), created in 2002, provides free access to children's books, in their original languages, over the internet. The ICDL Foundation's goal is to build a collection of books that represents outstanding historical and contemporary books from throughout the world. With children as design partners, an interdisciplinary team works with international experts in children's literature to make available an expanding collection of full-text historic and contemporary children's books. The mission of the Library is to encourage a love of reading, foster a readiness to learn, and offer a response to the challenges of world illiteracy.

At the time of writing the ICDL collection includes 2412 books in 41 languages. This is an interesting resource and you can search for books by continent and by title, author, or keyword, in dozens of languages. All the books in the ICDL can be sorted by title, author, illustrator, language, and publication date.

URL: **www.icdlbooks.org**

Letterbox Library

This London-based non-profit co-operative founded in 1983 provides multicultural and non-sexist books for children. This is a good source of American imports and the catalogue is particularly strong on picture books.

URL: **www.letterboxlibrary.com/acatalog/index.html**

Lovereading4kids.co.uk

This website features books for the 0–5 age range and useful 'like-for-like' author recommendations. The creators of the website say that Lovereading4kids has been created to be the ultimate children's online independent bookstore. Users need to register to use the site and an e-mail service keeps members up to date on the latest and best in their chosen age ranges. The message is that if young children have a favourite book or author, let them read it again and again, but also introduce a new author or book similar in style. The website creators also suggest that parents can enjoy online time with their children as much as watching TV with them.

Reading Is Fundamental (USA) – Leading to reading

This free, interactive resource is designed to help parents and childcare providers develop the language skills of their infants, toddlers and pre-school children. Available in English and Spanish, it includes stories, lullabies, finger games and nursery rhymes.

URL: **www.rif.org/leadingtoreading/en/babies-toddlers**

Their Reading Futures

'Picture Books for Storytelling with Young Children'; from the Their Reading Futures site:

URL: **www.theirreadingfutures.org.uk/documents/Early_years_story_time_book_list.rtf**

Stories from the Web

This is a reader development programme managed by Birmingham Libraries. The Early Years website is a pilot project funded by the Early Years Development Partnership Birmingham and aimed at 0-7 year olds. The website also has activities aimed at older age groups. The website is designed to develop language skills, confidence and an increased understanding of the world and aims to promote a love of reading from an early age. Using Stories from the Web will require guidance from an adult, as young children may need help in using the mouse and keyboard, explanation of what is happening on each page, or help with reading and writing. The five activity areas are: stories, writing, games, drawing and the gallery.

URL: **www.storiesfromtheweb.org/earlyyears/index.html**

The Word Pool

This website aims to increase the profile of UK children's books on the internet. It is a well established source of information for anyone interested in choosing or writing children's books. The Parents' Corner features books and links to help with parenting . This aims to be as comprehensive as possible and so includes the toughest part of parenting – caring for children who are unhappy, sick, disabled or emotionally scarred. In addition to books aimed at parents, the section includes reviews of some good children's fiction which may give parents an insight into their children's feelings. Users can sign up for a free monthly newsletter. The UK Children's Books Directory section provides links to the websites of a wide range of children's authors, illustrators, publishers and organizations.

URL: **www.wordpool.co.uk**

Equipment

Buyers' Guide Online is a useful source of information on library suppliers' products and services in the UK. Companies are listed alphabetically, by category and by the brand name of their products. The online service is supported by *The Annual Buyers' Guide Directory*, published in December of each year.

URL: **www.buyersguideonline.co.uk/**

Resources for bilingual books
Actionaid

Actionaid produces a range of multicultural books, teaching materials and resources to help teachers to bring a wide variety of cultures and traditions into the classroom. A catalogue is available on request.

URL: **www.actionaid.org.uk**

English with the Finglies CD-ROM

Designed for primary school children having their first contact with English, this features an animated story that presents language and simple grammatical structures in context. There are interactive activities, worksheets and flashcards, a teacher's guide CD-ROM, and reinforcement and extension exercises after each episode. All the material can be printed/photocopied as required. To download examples of the interactive exercises and teacher's guide visit the website. To order, or for more information, e-mail finglies@ydemas.com.

URL: **www.ydemas.com/finglies**

Fabula software

This software is designed to support bilingual literacy and allows teachers and children to create bilingual storybooks by inserting texts and scanned drawings or photographs into simple templates and adding special features of their own. The Fabula software, plus further information on the project and reading lists, is available free of charge on the website.

URL: **http://fabula. mozdev.org/**

The Global Dimension

This booklist from Leicestershire County Council Library Services for Education covers recent recommended multicultural fiction for ages 3+ to 16+. For details e-mail: lse@leics.gov.uk.

Issues and questions

- How can you develop and maintain a collection development plan for your early years library?
- Consider how to develop and share knowledge about diverse resources such as treasure baskets, toy libraries, storysacks and Bookstart packs.
- How can you provide a parenting collection to meet the needs of local families?

Key points to remember

- The selection of books and other resources is a key role for the early years librarian.
- You need to know the needs of your market before you can begin to provide the resources.
- In an early years collection, provide materials in a variety of formats to encourage play, creativity and development – the emphasis is on having fun.
- Collections are not just about books, as there are many ways to support literacy and the enjoyment of stories.

5

Reaching your audience – the librarian's role

Introduction

In this chapter we look at how the early years librarian can provide opportunities for young children and their families to enjoy literacy and language development activities together. In the UK the library service can be regarded as a key partner acting as a bridge to the community by providing a welcoming atmosphere. We discuss introducing a love of books to babies and young children and the role of stories and storytelling in helping to develop the imagination. Many early years librarians tell stories at sessions, providing entertainment and enlightenment for their local community. Acknowledging the skills required to effectively connect and engage with a family audience, we offer practical guidance for the librarian as performer. Continuing the theme of partnerships we discuss three examples of outreach work by looking at Traveller families, teenage fathers and culturally diverse communities. Partnerships are a key aspect of campaigns and promotional schemes and we look at some UK-based initiatives. The final section includes an example of programmes in use in Australia and the USA to provide library-based services to babies, young children and their families.

Providing a welcoming atmosphere

Librarians want to reach the family audience so as to encourage literacy skills and help build sustainable communities. The well planned early years library will provide a range of wonderful books, toys, treasure baskets and other creative resources for young users and their families. The environment in which these resources are offered also merits consideration, as audiences can be encouraged by sending positive messages. The early years librarian has an important role in helping children, and the adults with them, to feel comfortable and welcome in the library or early years setting. In planning a welcoming environment, children's craft and art work displayed on the walls can encourage links with the local community. In Chapter 3 we discussed how the physical aspects of the library can be planned to create a positive environment. In addition to the physical environment, the social atmosphere and ethos created by the library staff is an important factor in making families feel welcome. Encourage your colleagues to consider their behaviour and the non-verbal messages they send, particularly when feeling concerned about something. It can be difficult to show relaxed, positive body language all the time. It would be useful to promote discussions with other colleagues about how to manage certain challenging situations. Remember that babies may not always show model behaviour when they visit - they can be irritable and cranky when teething and will probably dribble! The more independent toddlers and pre-school children will look to adults for reassurance and guidance. The 'see me' stage of development can be irritating when your attention is demanded by boisterous youngsters - this isn't necessarily rude behaviour on the part of the child, but is how they check that the adults are paying attention. Guidance and training can help all staff to be aware of their own positive behaviour.

Libraries have a long history of providing services for their communities and we have mentioned the interest in supporting the reading child. With increased interest in providing the best start for very young children and their families, librarians are reaching out to the wider community. Miranda McKearney of The Reading Agency says 'the market opportunity is there for libraries to position themselves as the community hub for reading - social, lively, relevant' (2007, 40). We believe that libraries can reach their audiences by:

- modelling and encouraging parents to read with babies and young children from an early age

- providing a welcoming social space for families
- showing that parents are valued and that they are important as their child's first educator
- providing a variety of materials that can be borrowed, including multi-sensory, tactile books, story and information book, videos, DVDs and storysacks
- creating exciting book displays to encourage parents and children to select a range of different books
- providing activities such as colouring and drawing, story activities, singing, puppets, crafts
- having story sessions at times to suit parents and carers, including dads
- offering dual language story telling sessions and providing dual language books.

(Brock and Rankin, 2008, 29).

Introducing a love of books to babies, young children, parents and families

Reading to babies and young children and getting them involved with books is one of the most effective ways of enhancing language development. Babies can learn to handle books and acquire vocabulary, while parents and carers provide the words that match the pictures, using a range of sounds and beginning voice gymnastics with enthusiasm (Brock and Rankin, 2008, 27). Many books are quite tactile, with different materials to touch and feel, flaps to lift up or buttons to press, and these early book-handling experiences can be a very interactive and interesting process. Babies are our youngest scientists and they will explore books with their eyes, hands, mouths and feet.

Early literacy can be encouraged by sharing books, so let parents know that it is valuable to get into a routine with their baby. Each night before bed, it is good to choose a book together, whether a storybook or a simple text with pictures and just a few words on a page. For many parents it is helpful to know that reading before bed can settle the baby and ensure that there are fewer interruptions during the night. This time together is important, it will help to strengthen relationships and help the baby to feel relaxed and safe. Talk to Your Baby is a campaign run by the National Literacy Trust to encourage parents and carers to communicate more with their children from birth. We discuss this in more detail in Chapter 2, in the section on partnership with parents.

Early literacy was discussed in Chapter 1, but here are some further reminders about how parents can be supported by providing them with information on this aspect of the early years. Encouraging early literacy by sharing books is important because:

- it helps parent and child get to know each other better by supporting the bonding process
- it encourages the joys of reading from a very early age and generates a love of words, stories and how to gain information
- reading to a restless baby or young child can have a very calming effect
- a baby will begin imitating sounds and words when read to over a period of time
- learning how to handle books, and how to read from them, can help to develop a good educational foundation
- it helps to stimulate the imagination and an enquiring mind.

You can't start communicating with babies too soon, and early experiences are very valuable. Language-rich environments are important and reading to babies is one of the most effective ways of encouraging language (Brock and Rankin, 2008). Sharing books with babies and young children is a great way of helping them to learn to talk. Reading aloud combines the benefits of talking, listening and storytelling and helps to build the foundation for language skills. Reading stories to children is thought to be *the* most important activity for their reading capabilities on entry to school. You might also suggest some of the following read-aloud tips to parents and carers, provided by Reading is Fundamental USA. This guidance may also be useful information for staff in the early years library setting, as they will be interacting with families and can offer advice and encouragement:

- hold the baby in your lap; make sure he or she can see the pictures
- play with words, sing and make up rhymes; include the baby's name
- expect the baby to touch, grasp and taste, as that is how babies learn
- offer the baby a toy to hold and chew while listening to you read
- read one or two pages at a time; gradually increase the number of pages
- let the baby turn the pages if he or she is more interested in the book than in listening to you read; he or she will still be learning about books and enjoying your company
- point to, name and talk about things in pictures; describe what's happening
- ask the baby: 'Where's the . . .?' 'What's that . . .?' and wait for a response
- encourage the baby to join in - moo like a cow, or finish a repetitive phrase
- stay on a page as long as the baby is interested
- put the book away and do something else when the baby loses interest.

Using treasure baskets with babies

The concept of the treasure basket for babies was developed by Elinor Goldschmied as a method of play that helps babies and toddlers to learn naturally. We discussed the contents of treasure baskets and the development of these resources in libraries in Chapter 4. In contrast to the shared activity of reading books together, playing with a treasure basket is very much a baby-only activity. The parent's or carer's role is to provide security by having an attentive but not active presence. Encourage parents to sit and watch their babies enjoying the treasure basket without interfering. Parents should resist the temptation to choose objects that they think their baby would like; that is not what heuristic play - the active exploration of natural objects in a multi-sensory way - is about.

Goldschmied and Jackson (2004), explain that one of the things an adult may find difficult to do at first is not to intervene but to stay quiet and attentive. Sometimes a baby may quietly gaze at a treasure basket for some time before deciding to reach out and investigate an object. When two or three babies are seated round the treasure basket they will need close adult supervision and also protection from older mobile children. Babies are socializing when sharing a treasure basket. Though intent on handling their own chosen objects, babies are aware of each other, and for much of the time will be engaged in interactive exchanges. When planning the use of space in your early years library setting consider including a quiet, safe space that can be used for babies to be seated with the treasure baskets.

Using picture books

For our youngest children, pictures are their introduction to the world of books. In a picture book the illustrations are as important as the text. Picture books help young children to understand that words convey meaning, well before they are aware of the text. Picture books help to build vocabulary, an important building block for reading. Books can help young children to identify letters, shapes, numbers and colours, names of people, animals, places and everyday things. Picture books and illustrations encourage children's vocabulary development, as the adult supplies the word or words for pictures (as illustrated in Figure 5.1).

Picture books can also be a good starting point for adults with poor literacy skills or those trying to gain competence in a new language. Angela Robinson (n.d.) explained how the Picture This project in Blackburn with Darwen was designed to encourage adults with basic literacy skills to share books with their children. It can be embarrassing for people to admit to poor reading skill, but this can be avoided by using picture books and encouraging parents and carers to share them with their children. Proficiency in reading isn't necessary when using picture books, as the illustrations usually tell the stories. A key achievement in the Picture This project was actually encouraging local families to attend and it was important that the partner organizations working within the local children's centre helped with the promotion and publicity for the 6-week scheme.

The importance of picture books has been recognized in The Big Picture campaign. This is a Booktrust campaign to promote picture books and to

Figure 5.1 What can you see? Building vocabulary using picture books

expand the market for, increase the supply and enhance the status of picture books in the UK. Children's Laureate Michael Rosen is championing the campaign, saying that 'picture books are the fuse that lights our awareness that reading is full of intense pleasures'. To support the use of picture books in schools and early years settings, Booktrust has published *Looking at Books: The Big Picture Guide to exploring picture books* (2007).

Rhyme times

Rhyme time sessions provide a wonderful opportunity for parents and children to sing songs and rhymes together in an informal and supportive setting. These musical activities are enjoyed by families in children's libraries around the globe. Rhymes are a child-friendly way of introducing babies and toddlers to the wonder of narratives and the imaginative potential that the stories found in books can offer. The Early Years Foundation Stage (DfES, 2007)] indicates that you need to promote opportunities for children to:

- share and enjoy a wide range of rhymes, music, songs
- link language with physical movement in action songs and rhymes.

Rhyme, rhythm, songs and music are an important element of early language development. The importance of young children listening, singing and saying rhymes has been well researched and substantiated. This early knowledge eases children into early phonemic development and can make a real difference to beginning and developing reading skills. But rhymes are also important because they support children's sentence structure and vocabulary development. Young children can learn very complicated words through acquiring them in rhymes and songs. Rhymes also contribute to children's concept of story and to their pleasure in language for its own sake.

Children enjoy traditional rhymes and learn through them about sequences, events, motives, causes and effects (Cooper, 2004). Most cultures have their own long-established rhymes and they can be an important part of heritage and life experience. They are often based on everyday events and aspects of life such as washing day or the weather: 'Rain, rain go away'; 'Here we go round the mulberry bush'. Some nursery rhymes are set in the distant past and are historical sources: *Ring a ring of roses*; *Rock a bye baby* (a Caribbean lullaby); *The grand old Duke of York*.

Rhymes are fun and children love to sing and chant them. Do simple chants with babies. In the beginning they will not be able to pronounce all the words, but will jog along with the rhythm, gradually adding more and more words. Adults continue to model the correct words and with practice children become more and more competent and articulate. You can use:

- traditional rhymes
- nursery rhymes
- finger rhymes
- action rhymes
- counting rhymes
- humorous rhymes
- dual-language rhymes.

It is good fun to use the hand movements associated with many rhymes.

You can encourage shy children (and parents!) to join in by modelling the hand motions. Brock and Rankin (2008) describe how the staff at one children's centre created song and rhyme bags containing play resources and laminated song cards for *Five little ducks*, *Dr Foster went to Gloucester* and *Twinkle, twinkle little star* for parents and children to borrow for song activities at home. These bags contained visual and handleable resources to support children's learning of the songs and rhymes and to also extend the adults' repertoires. Having a range of these can broaden children's language and singing experiences, and also their cultural experiences. Songs in different home languages not only promote development of bilingualism, but are also a link to children's heritage. You should aim to involve parents and children in the singing, rhyming and reading of their culture's stories, songs and rhymes. Here are some English favourites:

- Incy Wincy Spider
- Old Macdonald had a farm
- Down in the jungle
- Jumping up and down on a big red tractor
- Clap your hands and wiggle your fingers
- Big red bus
- Two little dickie birds
- A baby is very tickly
- Wind my bobbin up
- Can you make a sound just like me?
- Zoom, zoom, zoom
- There's a spider on the floor
- Dingle dangle scarecrow
- Jumping Jack
- Five little bluebirds on my window
- Five little ducks
- Head, shoulders, knees and toes
- Five little monkeys
- Scrub a dub
- Miss Polly had a dolly
- Wide mouthed frog

- Peter Rabbit
- Eight little monkeys
- Roly Poly
- There was an old lady who swallowed a fly
- Row, row, row
- The wheels on the bus.

The early years librarians in Wakefield have produced tips for running successful rhyme times. To help build confidence, they begin each session with one familiar song that everybody will know. They aim to involve parents and carers right from the start of the rhyme time by encouraging them to join in with the singing and actions. Printed song sheets help everyone to participate and the programme is varied by using songs, spoken rhymes, tickle rhymes, action songs and simple books. Young children prefer a familiar routine, so don't worry if you sing the same songs every week. It is a good idea to use the same song each week as a signal that it's time to start the session, time for drinks, and tidy-up time at the end. In Chapter 6 we will look in more detail at the practical aspects of planning sessions.

Musical sessions – communicating through making music

Making music in the early years library is an activity that can easily involve parents. This should be a fun activity, and by exploring music and movement young children soon join in singing games and songs. You can create a treasure basket filled with different musical instruments and sound makers, such as spoons and pots. Music is a vehicle for expression and communication, just like language. You can try the following activities with babies as well as young children:

- create sound effects with your voice – whistling, humming
- use bodies to create sound – use hands, feet, chest, knees, head for clapping, stamping, clicking and banging
- beat out the rhythm and syllables of each child's name
- repeat sounds and get children to appreciate the rhythm of syllables within words

- make musical instruments – shakers containing rice, beans, seeds, marbles, buttons.

To encourage sound and song you can:

- create a bag of animals for Old MacDonald's farm
- put models of a spider, crocodile, cat and mouse in a bag and invite the children to select an object from the bag to prompt the song
- make songs personal for children by including their names in a song.

A 'Communicate through Music' activity pack has been jointly developed by Music one2one and Talk to Your Baby to encourage musical interaction with babies and young children. It is designed for practitioners and professionals, to help them to communicate the benefits of musical activities with parents and carers. The pack is designed to be a flexible resource and the materials can be freely copied and distributed. It includes the 'Babies Love Music' information sheet, which promotes the benefits of music and musical activities for use in your setting. Some libraries print this out to give to parents and carers.

Stories and storytelling

What's so important about storytelling? Well, stories are a means of learning about life. History, culture and family experiences are handed down through the generations by traditions of storytelling. New ideas, real-life issues and all sorts of characters can be explored and experienced through story. Listening to stories is an enjoyable experience and most adults and children are drawn into the listening process, whether it is one-to-one with an adult at home or in a group in your library. This is a great way to connect with your audience. Experience of stories helps everyone to understand the world in which we live, enabling us to make connections between what we are learning and what we already know. Swiniarski (2006), working in Salem in the USA, uses the concept of a 'global bookshelf' to promote a global education theme of unity and diversity.

Through using storytelling she aims for children to connect with others and to appreciate other cultures in an activity-based curriculum. The Early Years Foundation Stage (DfES, 2007) states that early years settings must offer opportunities for access to poetry, stories and non-fiction books and this advice holds true for libraries.

Remember that children like to hear favourite stories over and over again, as they enjoy the unchanging themes and find reassurance in familiar endings. They will often ask for the same bedtime story night after night and won't let you omit any of the pages! Parents can be assured that this is quite normal. For a good example of this, see Brock and Rankin (2008, 72), where the mum of three boys aged 2, 3 and 10 years talks about their bedtime routine and the importance of stories, particularly *We're Going on a Bear Hunt*, which they love to hear again and again. Children pay attention to rhythm and repetition, characters and events, words and meanings. There is so much to discover in a good story. Children will develop their abilities as readers, writers, storytellers and meaning makers from the stories they have heard. Listening to and reading stories from different genres is important, so consider the potential in your library setting for traditional fairy and folk tales, myths and legends, fantasy and adventure, fiction and non-fiction, family and animal stories.

> Storytelling is a powerful context for the development of the spoken word. Both storytelling and story reading are important for:
>
> - developing language
> - promoting vocabulary through rich description; providing exciting characters and events
> - organizing thought processes
> - offering complex narrative sequences
> - providing varied sentence structures
> - enjoying language for its own sake
> - most importantly, enjoying the story itself.
>
> (Brock and Rankin, 2008, 69)

It is important that staff working in a front-line role enjoy telling or reading stories. Carol Wootton, an experienced early years librarian from Wakefield, offers some practical advice on storytelling and using books:

> Children are not going to judge you on your storytelling skills, they are just quite happy to be read to or told a story. Moreover, if you do it every day you soon become an expert! Hence the importance of early literacy. It also doesn't matter if a parent cannot read, we need to encourage them just to talk about the pictures with their child, and maybe make up a story with their child about the pictures. It is important to talk to children about the books as well as reading to them; this helps them to develop a love of books.

The emphasis should be on having fun, but by providing prompts and support and asking key questions, adults and older children can assist in developing children's vocabulary and concepts. By posing problems and challenges you can encourage children to use their imaginations and develop their own storytelling skills. It is valuable to develop children's thinking through having conversations where there is equal interaction between adults and children and between children and children. Practitioners can help to create opportunities for 'sustained shared thinking' as described in the Effective Provision of Pre-School Education (EPPE) (DfES 1999–2002) and Researching Effective Pedagogy in the Early Years (REPEY) (DfES, 2002) research, which involves the adult being aware of the child's interests, and the adult and child working together to develop an idea or skill. From the librarian's perspective this means showing genuine interest by giving your whole attention, maintaining eye contact, affirming, smiling, nodding and offering encouragement. It also involves respecting children's opinions and choices and inviting them to elaborate by asking open questions. This supports and extends the children's thinking and helps to make connections in learning. In the most effective settings, practitioners support and challenge children's thinking by getting involved in the thinking process with them. Sustained, shared thinking can only happen when there are responsive, trusting relationships between adults and children (Potter, 2008, 59). It is useful to explain the importance of these interactive conversations to parents, and how story can be a very valuable way of developing 'storytelling' relationships and being imaginative with their children.

Families sharing stories

There is also much value in family stories that can be passed down the generations and family storytelling sessions are also a great way of involving grandparents. Invite families to contribute to your sessions by coming in to tell their stories, sharing them in writing, tape recording them or creating a booklet of stories.

The importance of families sharing storytelling is exemplified in the work of Storybook Dads, an independent charity which aims to maintain family ties and facilitate learning for prisoners and their children through story CDs. Based at Dartmouth Prison, the scheme started in 2002 and to date over 1700 prisoners have taken part. Any prisoner can record a story, regardless of their reading ability. The stories are digitally edited and sound effects and music are added. The children love these stories because they can hear their parent's voice whenever they want and this helps to maintain family ties.

This idea has been taken up by the armed forces and Storybook Soldiers was set up in 2007 to help provide a link between parents who are away on operations and their children. It is modelled on the Storybook Dad scheme; soldiers (both fathers and mothers are involved) are recorded reading a bedtime story and music and sound effects are added.

> We have delivered training to two army bases and an air force base. They now have editing suites up and running and are able to produce CDs for the children of service people. In 2008 we will be delivering training to the Navy. And so Storybook Soldiers, Storybook Squadrons and Storybook Sailors have been born!! (www.storybookdads.co.uk/indexnext.htm)

Stories in other languages – supporting the bilingual learner

The way a practitioner can structure stories through supporting bilingual children's language development in storytelling sessions can be very valuable. The adult can provide or model the language through storytelling while using props and 'this will enable children to gain confidence by repeating the vocabulary and language structures offered' (Brock and Power, 2007, 33). The children listen and feed the language back and these storytelling group activities can be very interactive and dramatic. There are valuable examples of how to do this using familiar stories such as *Elmer the Elephant*; *Farmer Duck*; *The Owl Babies*; *The Gruffalo* and *The Rainbow Fish* in Brock and Power (2007, 33 and 34). How to tell and read *The Three Billy Goats Gruff* in English and Hindi/Urdu is demonstrated in Brock and Rankin (2008, 39, 40 and 48). An extract from the story of *Send for Sohail* written in English and Urdu and how to use it with young children can be seen in Brock and Power (2007, 38–40).

Stories work with all children, but in particular with bilingual learners. It is very important to model the story, for the adults working with the children to actually become the Billy Goat, the Giant, Baby Bear. If we don't demonstrate, how can we expect the children to learn? An important tool is to 'shadow tell' the story: with the children playing roles, provide them with the words to repeat and they will expand upon them as they gain in confidence. Reading stories is fine, telling is fine, but neither of these is enough for children to become confident in using the words and phrases.

Using storysacks is a good way to support bilingual children (we discussed storysacks in detail in Chapter 4). Try to ensure that a range of stories from different cultures and backgrounds is available. Brock and Power (2006) suggest that one needs 'to be aware of the need to both affirm and extend the children – provide stories that they can see themselves in and stories that take them into environments other than their own' (2006, 3). Many schools and libraries are now using storysacks that they have either made with parents or bought from commercial suppliers. Many of these stories have repetitive language that enables the children to tell the story easily while handling the characters and props. The following stories are very suitable for use with a storysack:

- *Red Riding Hood* and other traditional tales
- *The Very Hungry Caterpillar*

- *Handa's Surprise*
- *Stone Soup*
- *Topiwalo the Hatmaker*
- *Mrs Wishy Washy*
- *Where the Wild Things Are*
- *Mr Gumpy's Outing*
- *Sandeep and the Parrots*
- *Send for Sohail*

(Brock and Power, 2007, 37).

Strategies for sharing stories with children – the librarian as performer
Ideas for making up stories in your library

There are so many wonderful story books available that you may have a difficult time choosing which ones to read aloud! Alternatively you may feel confident to make up stories involving your own library setting. Carol Wootton from the Bookworms Library in Wakefield offers some practical advice:

> If you feel confident about making up your own stories and see a scenario that you think could be used in storytelling with children, then jot it down in case you forget it. Many situations can be turned into stories for children. For example, if you are telling a story in a library, you can pretend that you have a resident animal that hides there, perhaps a mouse, rabbit or even a teddy. Tell the children what this little resident gets up to once the library has closed. Leave his little footprints around for the children to find – that makes it even more realistic for them! One week you can get the children to draw pictures for him and in the following week let them find a thank-you note from him. It can be great fun thinking up little adventures, and they don't have to last long, especially with younger children. You can plan to have a particular ending to your stories or leave them open ended and ask the children for their version of the ending. It is a fun thing to do.

As the teller, you must enjoy the story and want to share it with your young audience. There are a number of things to bear in mind when taking the storyteller role. You can:

1   Use props, costume and story resources to help set the scene.
2   Make use of your voice and of rhythm and tenor to create pace, surprise, suspense and anticipation.
3   Use gestures and movement to create effects of size, space, weather, action.
4   Pay special attention to how you portray your characters. Good characters bring a story to life, so put life into them with facial expressions, voice, gestures and body posture. You can characterize using intonation, emphasis, accent and dialect. Try to make each character different enough that they're easily told apart. When portraying two characters talking together try a 'cross-focus' technique where you make each one face a different 45-degree angle.
5   Tell and retell favourite parts of the story or repeat some sections for effect or comprehension.
6   Involve the children in telling and acting out the story.
7   Include children's names so that they feel they are part of the story (this can also be a good way to hold their attention and involvement).
8   Incorporate personal and shared information about the local community to further develop a story.

It is a good idea to assess the children's listening abilities and engagement in the story. Young children do not have very long attention spans, so use ways of gaining and holding their attention. Try to maintain eye contact with your audience – this also gives you a chance to see what they are doing and how engaged they are! Some traditional storytellers will sit in a special seat – there is a storyteller's chair and a storytelling cloak in the Artist's Attic at Seven Stories, the Centre for Children's Books in Newcastle-upon-Tyne. Sue Wiggins, early years librarian at the Airedale Library and Family Centre in Castleford, wears a storytelling hat for her early years story time sessions. You could also use artefacts such as a magic carpet, an enchanted lamp, story wand or crystal ball.

Voice projection and performance skills

Some of us will have no problem at all in telling or reading stories aloud to an audience. Others will feel very nervous about the idea of a public performance - even if it is to a group of babies and their parents. Certain approaches and techniques will help you to prepare and have confidence in telling and reading stories and using your voice. Practise breathing deeply and correctly to project and sustain your voice. To check this, place your hand on your stomach. As you inhale and your lungs expand, you should feel your stomach push out. Many people do the opposite, holding in their stomachs and breathing only with their upper chests. Try to keep your back straight, so your lungs can expand fully. Don't push your voice too hard or use it unnaturally except when speaking as characters in the story. Practise using different, exaggerated character voices. During the storytelling performance try to relax your body, especially your throat and jaw muscles.

There are other practical things you can do to enhance the storytelling performance. This is about creating the right atmosphere and ensuring your young audience are engaged. Wearing a storyteller's hat or a story cloak can help to you assume the 'role' and play the part with confidence.

Reading aloud techniques – Mem Fox's Ten Commandments

Mem Fox is an Australian writer who has championed early literacy for many years. Her *Read Aloud Commandments* have been included here as they are practical, humorous and also effectively summarize the message we want to share about reading stories out loud. The guidance is aimed at anyone involved with children, but you can reflect on how you feel about reading aloud in your library setting. Reading aloud is an effective way to connect with your young audience.

1 Spend at least ten wildly happy minutes every single day reading aloud.
2 Read at least three stories a day: it may be the same story three times. Children need to hear a thousand stories before they can begin to learn to read.
3 Read aloud with animation. Listen to your own voice and don't be dull,

or flat, or boring. Hang loose and be loud, have fun and laugh a lot.

4 Read with joy and enjoyment: real enjoyment for yourself and great joy for the listeners.

5 Read the stories that the kids love, over and over and over again, and always read in the same 'tune' for each book: i.e. with the same intonations on each page, each time.

6 Let children hear lots of language by talking to them constantly about the pictures, or anything else connected to the book; or sing any old song that you can remember; or say nursery rhymes in a bouncy way; or be noisy together doing clapping games.

7 Look for rhyme, rhythm or repetition in books for young children, and make sure the books are really short.

8 Play games with the things that you and the child can see on the page, such as letting kids finish rhymes, and finding the letters that start the child's name and yours, remembering that it's never work, it's always a fabulous game.

9 Never ever teach reading, or get tense around books.

10 Please read aloud every day, mums and dads, because you just love being with your child, not because it's the right thing to do.

(www.memfox.net/ten-read-aloud-commandments.html)

Puppets

Another way of connecting with your young audience and their families is to use puppets. When telling stories it can be great fun to have story aids such as puppets as they give your young audience something visual to focus on. Puppets can be used by adults to tell stories to children and by children to tell stories themselves They are a great way to engage an audience as they can encourage older children to chat, discuss the story lines and offer advice on the outcomes and consequences. Children can emotionally engage with the puppets. If you are storytelling without a book, a puppet is a good prop to use. They don't have to be expensive and Carol Wootton suggests that home-made puppets work as well as any others:

Don't be afraid to use props such as puppets or a soft toy. I have a storybear that the children look after while I'm reading stories. Some people like to use

puppets to give them confidence, because the children tend to look at the puppet rather than you. If you are good at doing voices you can make the puppet
speak to the children, or you can have a silent puppet that whispers in your
ear. It's not something you have to do; it's how comfortable you feel.

Staff at the Shadsworth Children's Centre in Blackburn with Darwen used
a puppet theatre to stage a performance of *Sleeping Beauty* as part of a
monthly reading group project to encourage adults with basic literacy to
share books with their children.

Reaching 'hard to reach' audiences

The phrase of 'hard to reach' is used by 'government and other agencies to
describe some groups, their families and children that are less likely than others
to be using early years services' (Lane, 2008, 83). Care must be taken when
using this term, as it can have negative connotations and Lane (2008, 84)
suggests that if services can consider 'whether they themselves are easy to
reach', some of the potential barriers might be more easily broken down.

It is recognized that librarians are good at reaching 'hard to reach'
groups, particularly when offering services that promote social inclusion
(Stevens, 2003). LISU (the Library and Information Statistics Unit based
at Loughborough University) collects data annually on a wide range of library
activities and includes the extent of outreach services undertaken by
public libraries. Where practitioners are tackling social exclusion, you
may need to justify outreach time away from the library setting. It is a
question of balance between making the library service as accessible and
as appropriate as possible to the wider community and maintaining a
quality service for those who actually visit the library. Their Reading
Futures provides guidance on reader development through work beyond
the library walls; this includes gathering evidence of success with your
targeted groups. Further information can be found on the website at
www.thereadingfutures.org.uk. The next sections look at how libraries
are promoting outreach work, using three examples: Traveller families,
teenage fathers and culturally diverse communities. It is interesting to
note that this challenging outreach work is often most effectively

accomplished by using the power of partnerships with other key organizations.

Traveller, Roma and Gypsy families

Outreach is a fundamental aspect of working with Traveller, Roma and Gypsy families. Traveller Education Support Services (TESS) operate in most local authorities to improve access to education and other services for the children and families in these communities. Outreach can mean bringing families into existing local services or delivering a service directly to a family who have no means of access. These families may remain excluded from many mainstream services and opportunities, particularly health and education, as a service is effectively closed to someone who does not know about it and who has no relationship with it. Children may miss out on the Bookstart gifts, especially if their families are highly mobile. Libraries have been proactive in helping to reach these groups. Riches (2007) reports on storytelling services for the under-fives being made available on mobile libraries, and Sure Start librarians have arranged for book boxes to be given to Traveller communities. In some areas where there is no mobile library, the local library has arranged open days specifically for families from the Gypsy and Traveller communities. These open days allow the families to come together and be assisted to register as library users and find out what is available. In another example of outreach services, the Oswestry Sure Start Children's Centre has a mobile play bus with an on-board toy library service that visits sites, and the Sure Start librarian has organized story time sessions on site and a library box for 0–5 year olds. The library service in Essex and the Essex Travellers' Education Service are bringing books to families living on Traveller sites in the county. Mobile libraries make weekly stops at a number of sites and also at primary schools with a high proportion of Traveller pupils. Preparation for this project included cultural awareness training for librarians and careful selection of stock covering subjects known to be of interest to the Traveller community, such as non-fiction books on animal husbandry.

A number of key organizations, including the Society of Chief Librarians, have collaborated to make it easier for Travellers to return library materials, thus removing one of the barriers to the use of libraries by people who are on the move. Children and young people who are Travellers, looked after, refugees or asylum seekers (and their parents or carers) can return library materials to any library in the UK without any overdue charges being made. The receiving library will make arrangements to return the items to the originating library free of charge (The Network, press release January 2006).

Teenage fathers

It is important that fathers are involved in interacting with their babies and form close relationships through playing with, chatting to, singing songs and telling stories with them. Sherriff (2007) has written about supporting fathers in developing positive relationships with their children. Significant barriers can make engagement difficult, e.g. cultural issues, negative perceptions of young fatherhood, and poor referral systems. The need for projects agencies and services supporting young fathers to adopt a planned approach to their work is stressed as is the importance of networking and developing partnerships with other agencies and organizations in order to increase the chances of successful outcomes for young fathers, their children and their families (**www.youngfathers.net**).

In an example of good practice, a successful partnership in Leeds is encouraging teenage fathers to engage positively with their children. Leeds Library and Information Services support the Leeds Teenage Pregnancy and Parenthood Strategy and are working with Fact (Fathers and children together) to provide sessions that are both engaging and of benefit to the young fathers and their children. These evening sessions are held in Leeds Central Library and the Fact team accompany the teenage fathers and their children to the library. The Bookstart and Rhyme Time session encourages the fathers to read to their children and the group made musical instruments as part of the musical activity. This session also provides an opportunity for the young fathers to collect the free Bookstart packs for their babies. The follow up session 'Library Tour and Digital Photography Time' encourages the group to interact with their children by taking photographs and learning to use Photoshop to edit the pictures. Feedback from the young fathers and 'Fathers and children together' group has been very positive.

Culturally diverse communities

In today's society, particularly in, but not only in, inner city areas, refugees, asylum seekers and economic migrants all need support services. Outreach workers from a variety of agencies are involved in providing these services. Such services need thoughtful marketing approaches, as it is important to encourage the communities and their families to access what is available to them. There are barriers to using local resources, including lack of knowledge about availability of and access to resources in the UK, misconceptions that using services may have financial implications and language difficulties. It may therefore be necessary to take these services, including library provision, out to the communities themselves, and experienced outreach workers can make a real difference.

Case study

Bilingual Library Outreach in Bradford

The following statements made by parents to the bilingual outreach workers are about library outreach work in Bradford. They show how a lending library of toys and books for young children of playgroup age is highly valued by the community. The adults state how they love the storybook lending scheme and feel that they have become more confident in reading books to their children.

> I feel my daughter is learning very quickly and she always wants to play with her dad and me. I read books with her all the time, especially at bedtime.

> I always read books now with my child, whereas before I was afraid to take him to the library because he would tear the books. Since attending these sessions he can now handle the books properly and is more eager to share the books with other children and adults.

> I always borrow books and enjoy reading with my child. It has made me feel more confident to play with my child and given me more ideas about different ways of playing with children.

I look at books with him. We go to the library – he enjoys going to the library. He chooses his own books and reads. He always wants me to sit down and read to him. He tries really hard and uses the pictures to create his own stories, completely different from the actual story.

At first I was very shy to read to my son in public. I had to be on my own when I read to him, where no one was listening and looking. I am more confident now and don't mind reading to him in front of other people.

Although I can't speak English I do help her look at books and tell the story in my own language and also we talk about the things that are going on in the book and tell the story that way.

It is very useful and we take a lot of books and toys home. It is useful because we don't have a lot of different things for her at home.

We think these statements by parents and carers are most interesting and valuable – they provide real insight into how much can be gained by encouraging families to access library services.

Promotions and campaigns in early years libraries

Campaigns and promotions are used by businesses to market products and services to particular audiences or target groups. Incentives are often offered to encourage the target group to take up the idea suggested by the marketing. In this sense, libraries can also be regarded as businesses, and national campaigns can be used to raise awareness of particular services and opportunities on offer. This section discusses some of the promotional campaigns libraries can use to reach out to the early years audience in the local community. Some of these are annual events that are part of a much wider community; others are an integral part of the ongoing business of the early years library setting. A connecting theme is the importance of working in partnerships.

National Reading Campaign

The National Reading Campaign (NRC) aims to ensure that as many people as possible enjoy the pleasures and benefits that reading can bring. It is delivered by the National Literacy Trust on behalf of the DfCSF and is part of the legacy of the first UK National Year of Reading, 1998–9. The National Reading Campaign is the collective name for a number of initiatives, including the Family Reading Campaign, which is helping to make every home a reading home. This partnership campaign wants the encouragement of reading in the home to be integrated into the activity of key sectors. The NRC promotes reading for pleasure throughout the community, to demonstrate the varied ways in which reading can inspire and sustain people to develop their skills, with a focus on those most in need. The NRC also provides a network to bring the reading community together and maximize support for reading events. Its website provides information on effective ways of promoting reading. The National Literacy Trust is now working on a government-sponsored proposal to develop the Family Reading Campaign into a national strategy to support families and encourage literacy in the home (NLT, 2007b).

National Year of Reading

The National Year of Reading (NYR) 2008 is about celebrating and encouraging reading in all its forms. Led by the National Literacy Trust on behalf of the DfCSF, NYR supports ongoing work to achieve national literacy targets, engage parents and families in reading with their children and develop adult literacy. The year's key values are diversity, creativity and partnership. Every library authority in England has committed to NYR and has planned promotional events: reading anytime, anyplace, anything. The focus on reading provides a great opportunity for early years librarians to promote activities and sessions to encourage family reading.

Bookstart Book Crawl

Libraries want to appear welcoming to the very youngest members of their communities. The Bookstart Book Crawl is a library-joining incentive for children aged 0–4 years. It encourages children under five to join the library and to borrow books by rewarding them with stickers and certificates. Birmingham Libraries encourage their youngest members to book crawl by the enticing message 'There are great selections of gorgeous picture books to borrow including plenty of hardwearing board books to withstand sticky hands and sharp teeth!'

Scenario: A reading milestone for Baby Ella

One bright spring morning Ella, aged 9 months, brought her mother, grandmother and aunt to the new Bookworms Library at Pinmoor Children's Centre in Wakefield. The baby was excited and looked around with wide eyes as she sat with her mum on the soft carpet. Ella bobbed her head in happiness and blew bubbles back at mum. Grandmother and aunt sat on adult-size chairs and looked on with pleasure, glancing around the brightly coloured library taking in all the toys, books and other playthings on display. This was an important day for the family, as they had come to celebrate with Ella. As one of the youngest members of the new Bookworms Library, the baby had reached the first of many milestones as a reader: she had achieved her first Book Crawl certificate. Carol, the early years librarian, sat on the carpet and presented Ella with her award. Mum smiled, grandmother and aunty laughed and clapped, Ella showed her delight by immediately sucking the edge of her certificate. We took a photograph. A snapshot moment – hopefully a lifetime of literacy ahead.

Chatterbooks groups

Older children, aged 4–12 years, are supported through the Chatterbooks national network of reading groups in libraries. Co-ordinated by The Reading Agency, the Chatterbooks scheme reaches families who may not have had a connection with libraries before and the reading groups promote access to all kinds of learning in the community, both for the young people who join and for their parents and carers. Every child joining a Chatterbooks group gets a pack with a reading diary, Post-It review pads, games and stickers. Library authorities who have signed up to deliver the scheme can access the Chatterbooks resources section on Their Reading Futures website.

World Book Day

World Book Day has been designated by UNESCO as a worldwide celebration of books and reading, and is marked in over 100 countries around the globe. It is a partnership of publishers, booksellers and interested parties who work together to promote books and reading for the personal enrichment and enjoyment of all. World Book Day (WBD) entered its second decade in the UK and Ireland in 2008 and the initiative is well established in schools and libraries. The WBD happens in school term time (Thursday 5 March in 2009) to help make the most of the opportunity to celebrate books and reading; other countries celebrate World Book Day on 23 April every year. In the UK and Ireland the core activities involve schools and pre-school settings, with children receiving World Book Day book tokens. A main aim is to encourage children to explore the pleasures of books and reading by providing them with the opportunity to have a book of their own. The WBD event also offers a great opportunity for a wide range of reading and story- telling activities. Many schools and early years library settings celebrate World Book Day by having a dressing-up day, with both children and adults dressing as characters in their favourite book or story. Some settings provide reading tents with books and storysacks, others organize book sales, book donations and group sharing of favourite books. The WBD website provides a range of pre-school resources, including downloadable colouring and activity sheets.

A look elsewhere – early years activities in other countries

Early years library provision is also delivered by partnerships in other parts of the world. In this section we take a brief look at two examples from Australia and the USA.

Australia – Better Beginnings

The UK's Bookstart programme has been used as a model in Western Australia. Better Beginnings is an early literacy project co-ordinated by the Western Australian State Library and forms part of the Western Australian Government's early years strategy. Launched state-wide in 2005, it aims to inform parents of their role as their child's first teacher. North and Allen (2005) explain how the programme strategies are delivered through partnership working and how a project co-ordinator from the State Library of Western Australia provides advice and support to project partners. A resource pack is given to parents of young babies at their 6-weeks check up. This contains a quality children's book, a growth measurement chart, information about the value of reading to children, some titles of popular books and information about local library resources. Parent-and-child workshops and baby story time sessions are held at the local library. These activities involve young children, their parents, health and child development professionals and librarians. Research has shown that Better Beginnings has had a significant impact on indigenous and culturally and linguistically diverse (CALD) communities (Rohl and Barratt-Pugh, 2006).

Better Beginnings spreads the message that sharing books and stories with even the smallest babies and very young children has a positive impact on literacy development. It's also an opportunity for libraries to contribute in yet another positive way to the communities they serve. Expansion of the scheme includes targeted strategies for 'hard to reach' and special needs communities, including indigenous and remote communities. Family Reading Centres have been established in a number of public libraries and aim to bring together resources for parents and children in one place within the public library, making it easier for young families to browse for resources, with activities and toys close by to entertain their children.

USA – Family Place Libraries

Family Place Libraries™ is a network of children's librarians in the USA who believe that literacy begins at birth, and that libraries can help build healthy communities by nourishing healthy families. This is a joint initiative of Middle Country Public Library and Libraries for the Future, and at the time of writing the network included more than 220 sites in 23 states. Feinberg and Rogoff explain that 'The Family Place project takes a holistic and developmentally informed approach to the promotion of emergent literacy and healthy child development by addressing the needs of children at the earliest stages, and supporting the role of parent as a child's first and most important teacher' (1998, 50).

Family Place Libraries redesign the library environment to be welcoming and appropriate for children, beginning at birth. The services offered at the library and other family service agencies reach out to non-traditional library users. This creates the network families need to nurture their children's development during the critical first years of life and helps to ensure that all children enter school ready and able to learn.

It is interesting to note that, according to Kropp (2004), the core components of a Family Place Library are:

- Collections of books, toys, music and multimedia materials for babies, toddlers, parents and service providers
- A specially designed, welcoming space within the children's area for families with young children
- The parent/child workshop which is a five week program that involves toddlers and their parents and caregivers; features local professionals who serve as resources for parents; emphasizes the role of parents as the first teachers of their children; facilitates early intervention; and teaches strategies for healthy child development and early literacy
- Coalition-building with community agencies that serve families and young children to connect parents to community resources and develop programs and services tailored to meet local needs
- Outreach to new and non-traditional library users, especially parents and very young children (beginning at birth)
- Developmentally appropriate programming for very young children and their parents
- Library staff trained in family support, child development, parent education and best practices.

(Kropp, 2004)

It is also interesting that the Family Place Library network provides specific training packages for the library staff involved in the scheme. Further information is available at **www.familyplacelibraries.org/whatMakes.html**.

Final comments

There is a wealth of initiatives in operation, both in the UK and overseas, and only some of them have been listed in this chapter. Do make time to visit the sources mentioned and glean further insights and ideas for professional practice. Also make time to search on the web to discover more information, as in this way you can learn from what others are doing. Be proactive in contacting the agencies and organizations mentioned.

Issues and questions

- Do a critical review of the resources and activities provided in your library setting.
- Do the books in your setting reflect diversity in terms of genre, heritage and format?
- How can you use campaigns and promotions to market your services and connect with 'hard to reach' audiences?

Key points to remember

- Early story experiences can make a huge difference to language development and stories and books are the routes into literacy.
- Cater for all age groups through providing a range of resources and activities.
- Entice everyone into your library setting – babies, toddlers, young children, parents and carers (including dads) – home and away; communities and businesses.

Useful organizations

Better Beginnings (Australia), **www.better-beginnings.com.au**
Family Place Libraries (USA),
   www.familyplacelibraries.org/whatMakes.html

Library and Information Statistics Unit,
   www.lboro.ac.uk/departments/ls/lisu
National Reading Campaign,
   www.nationalliteracytrust.org.uk/campaign/index.html
Seven Stories, the Centre for Children's Books,
   www.sevenstories.org.uk

6

Planning

Introduction

The theme in this final chapter is planning. All organizations, and indeed individuals, need to plan for their future success and sustainability. Planning is a vital activity at all levels and we discuss some of the issues associated with planning in organizations and multidisciplinary teams. Financial planning is discussed as a very important means of allocating resources to enable development. We also look at some practical aspects of project planning, as many early years librarians have opportunities to set up schemes and initiatives, often in partnership work. Impact and evaluation are also discussed, as these are important stages in the planning cycle for any project or activity. As a main theme in this book is early years literacy and the enjoyment of books, we have included a section on planning sessions for babies, young children and their families. The final sections look at planning at the individual level and we discuss aspects of continuous professional development (CPD) and developing skills for the reflective practitioner.

Organizational planning – strategic, tactical, operational

To be an effective early years practitioner and to undertake a planning role in the workplace, it is helpful to understand the ways in which your parent organization and library and information services work. In most organizations the senior managers lead formal strategic planning processes to determine long-term plans, strategies and direction for the business. In the not-for-profit sector in the UK, organizations and agencies will consider how to meet the requirements of government agendas such as Every Child Matters, Early Years Foundation Stage and The Children's Plan. Some of these current issues are discussed in Chapter 1.

The purposes of an organization are often expressed through its mission statement and corporate aims, which are then broken down into more specific objectives. Table 6.1 shows the characteristics associated with different levels of purpose in a typical hierarchical organization:

Table 6.1 Levels of purpose in an organization	
Level of purpose	**Common characteristics**
Mission	Visionary and far-reaching
	Central and over-riding
	Sometimes implicit, i.e. unwritten
Corporate (strategic) aims	Identify goals for the whole organization
	Formulated by senior management
	Set stakeholder expectations
	Often expressed in terms of 'market share'
Unit (operating) objectives	Identify goals specific to units of organization
	Practical and operational
	Reflected in activities and tasks of the unit
	Expressed in terms of 'outcomes' or 'outputs'

Another way of expressing this activity is by means of basic questions. At the strategic management level the question is 'Why?' This most senior level carries overall accountability for the success of the organization. Staff working at this level will determine the mission and the corporate aims by undertaking long-term planning and strategic development. When the direction for the organization has been determined the next basic question is 'How will the corporate aims be achieved?' The 'how' question is implemented by managers operating at a tactical level in the hierarchy. They will interpret aims at the level of the business unit and undertake medium-term planning to achieve the objectives of the organization. This level of management has a co-ordinating role and often controls systems and resources. Further down the hierarchy, operational managers are responsible for delivering what needs to be done on a day-to-day basis and who needs to do it. Operational targets are usually short term and monitoring is done at local task level. The overall process should ensure that the organization achieves its objectives, with everyone in the organization involved. This is a very simplistic overview of an organizational structure, but has been included to help explain the potential challenges in partnership work.

SMART objectives

If objectives are to be useful in helping an organization move towards achieving its goals they need to be clearly understood by everyone working towards that end. One way of doing this is to set SMART objectives. This stands for Specific, Measurable, Attainable, Realistic and Timely. These criteria can be used to evaluate how useful an organization's objectives actually are:

- Specific - clearly identifiable and focused, as the organization needs to know what exactly it is trying to achieve
- Measurable - the organization needs to know whether the objective has been achieved or exceeded, or how far short it is falling
- Achievable - the organization needs to ensure that the resources (skills, funds, time) necessary to achieve the objective are provided
- Realistic - those who must work to achieve the objective must feel that the expectations of managers are realistic
- Timely - a deadline should be set by which the objective must be achieved, or when progress towards it will be assessed.

When describing your work plans as a series of objectives it can be helpful to use this approach.

The challenges of partnership work - planning shared objectives

We have already identified that partnership working is seen as an important strategy for tackling complex issues such as social inclusion and supporting the lifelong learning agenda. Many UK workplace settings now require services or projects to be delivered by a series of teams, each team a multi-disciplinary one made up of professionals from different backgrounds. Partnership working can present challenges and barriers, particularly in cross-sector partnerships where participants are from different organizations and agencies. Some of the difficulties may involve having different strategic objectives and priorities, working to different time frames, or differences in organizational culture. Practical difficulties, such as differences in systems and procedures, may be quite frustrating at an operational level.

On a positive note, Allan (2007) identifies many benefits from working in partnership, based on her discussions with directors of library and information services and project managers. These include enhanced access to people, resources and organizations and ownership of projects. The involvement of a wide range of people from different professional backgrounds can enhance the quality of the project outcomes. Being part of a successful partnership can boost morale. Individuals working on a collaborative project will have the opportunity to develop their knowledge and skills through teamwork and this will enhance continuing professional development.

Planning and organizing projects

What is a project? In contrast to managing and delivering your core services, which are financed on a recurring basis, a project may be expected to have the following features:

- a clearly defined set of objectives or outputs
- a specific start and end date
- involve the investment of resources for future benefit
- can be planned, financed and implemented as a unit
- geographical or organizational boundaries.

A project is different from managing and delivering core services, which are managed on a recurrent, ongoing basis. A new service may have been initiated as a trial project to get it up and running. Early years library practitioners may be involved in capital projects involving new buildings, moving into a new early years setting or perhaps refurbishing an existing setting. Other practical examples might be developing a marketing campaign for the library, setting up a new parenting collection in a branch library or running a storysack workshop for the local community.

Managing projects involves using various management skills and activities, such as:

- carrying out some research to identify gaps in provision
- setting objectives to decide what is to be achieved within a specified timescale
- developing a plan to decide what needs to be done and in what order
- allocating resources and managing the people in order to achieve the objectives of the project
- communicating with the stakeholders – disseminating information about the progress and the outputs
- evaluating the project against the set objectives.

Organizations need to consider the staffing resources that will be involved in running the project and the management systems and structures required to deliver the outputs. These will depend on the size and complexity of the project. A small-scale project is sometimes run as a pilot or a trial to test out a new service idea and gain feedback before rolling it out on a full scale. Allan (2004) has written about project management tools and techniques for information and library practitioners. Teamwork is vital.

Projects to be delivered by multidisciplinary teams can fail because of a lack of clarity about the objectives. Where team members do not share a common goal, there is likely to be a conflict of interests. It is a good idea to involve all partners in planning from the start. Senior managers may need to be persuaded that projects need dedicated time from co-ordinating members to ensure successful outputs.

Action plans can be used in projects to show who is doing what and the timescale involved. Gantt charts, laid out on a grid, are helpful for project management because they show the project schedule and associated tasks at a glance. A Gantt chart shows the time phases and activities of a project so that they can be understood by a wide audience. Specialized project management software is used when there is a high level of complexity, but you can use an Excel spreadsheet or the table feature in Microsoft Word to create a basic outline for planning needs. Gantt charts are easy to read and can be used to show recurrent tasks and milestones. In simple projects you can very effectively use a whiteboard or flip-chart paper and Post-It notes for the same purpose.

Table 6.2 is an example of a simple Gantt chart showing the scheduling of tasks and the timescales involved in planning a storysack workshop for a local community.

Table 6.2 Gantt chart – scheduling a storysack project

Task	January	February	March	April	May	June
Planning meeting with partner organizations to agree storysack theme and to allocate budget and staffing	■					
Book activity room for the workshop	■					
Order resources – books, sewing materials etc.		■	■			
Produce publicity material and advertise event			■	■		
Brief staff and plan workshop session Prepare resource materials				■	■	
Order refreshments for the workshop				■		
Issue press release, invite local paper/radio station to provide coverage on the day					■	
Run the workshop Gather evaluation evidence					■	
Prepare evaluation report for partner organizations						■

Planning budgets and money matters in the early years library

Budgeting involves the allocation of resources among the competing activities, programmes and services provided by an organization. Put simply, this can be seen as a series of goals with price tags. Operating or revenue budgets are terms used to describe year-by-year budgets, generally drawn up on an annual basis to fund current operations. A different budget source, the capital budget, will be used for high-cost improvements or major purchases such as a new building. Another type of budget is the single-purpose grant from government agencies, commercial partners or charitable foundations. These special budgets are often allocated on a competitive basis, may have varying time periods and could include both capital and operating funds. Collaborative partnerships often attract this form of finance and your parent organization may be involved in such schemes. Funding available for special projects usually has to be allocated and used within specific timescales and may need to be treated separately for accounting and auditing purposes.

Budget headings for the everyday running of an early years library might typically include:

- staffing/payroll costs
- accommodation costs; rents, cleaning, heating and lighting
- books and other resources such as DVDs and videos
- toys and play equipment, treasure baskets
- craft materials and other stationery
- magazines and newspapers for the parenting collection
- staff development and training
- publicity and marketing
- office supplies and consumables
- IT equipment
- library management system, including maintenance contracts
- projects and programmes
- travel and subsistence for outreach work.

Financial management in information and library services is very important and the future success of a library service may be dependent on the effective planning, organization and control of the financial resources. You cannot afford to neglect financial matters and, according to Roberts (1998), improving budgetary practice should be seen as a strategic goal of all information and library service managers. In the present economic climate it is not enough to ensure that expenditure is kept within budget, as managers are generally expected to provide the best level of performance for the available finance and may have cost targets and income targets as part of the process. Library managers are now required to justify expenditure on particular items or for the whole service, and Corrall reminds us:

> Most information service managers are faced with decreasing financial and human resources, but increasing customer demands and wider delivery options, requiring complex decision making, which in turn requires effective management information systems - particularly information on costs.
>
> (Corrall, 2000, 166-7)

Library practitioners need to take responsibility for developing their own knowledge and skills in financial management and encouraging staff working with them to do the same. All practitioners should be aware of the financial context in which they work and have some knowledge of the financial performance indicators on which their services are judged. The ability to cost activities has become more important with diminishing resources and increasing accountability, but an inherent problem for libraries is that the work is very labour intensive. Roberts (1998) suggests that many performance measures are incomplete if a financial dimension cannot be included.

Budgets can have several purposes, both as plans for the distribution of resources and as tools for the prediction of costs. At one level the budget for your early years library service can be your action plan expressed in financial terms, and this can act as a control mechanism and an evaluation tool for your activities. Viewed another way, the budget has a role in the translation of your organization's strategic plans into practical, everyday service delivery outcomes. Practical wisdom suggests that you should keep a close eye on your budgets and commit funds well before the end of the financial year. Experienced practitioners will keep a wish list - when a tranche of money becomes available you have to take the opportunity and allocate it quickly.

Planning library sessions

In planning library sessions for the early years audience there are some practical things to consider. Publicity and advertising are important to ensure your target market know what is on offer and where. In planning the structure of your session consider how long it will last and what format it will take. The venue also needs to be factored into the plan as this will affect the activities you can undertake and the resources readily available – are you holding the sessions in the children's library or in a separate room in a library building, or are you going out into the community? It is a good idea to have a theme for a story session, such as numbers, weather, animals, colours, holidays, magic and enchantment, pets or nursery rhymes. Some library authorities have produced themed resource packs containing books, rhymes and song sheets, musical instruments, puppets, games, CDs and cassettes. These can be shared by a number of early years librarians. It is also a good idea to plan the beginnings and endings of your sessions. Infants and young children respond well to what is familiar and so it is a good idea to begin and end each session with the same simple songs. Some venues have a welcome song such as:

Hello Everybody
Hello everybody, how do you do?
How do you do? How do you do?
Hello everybody, how do you do?
How do you do today?

The Reading Agency has provided an extensive checklist of 'Hints for Reading to Under 5s', including practical guidance such as coming to the story time with more books than you need – all of them stories which you like and have practised reading out loud. It is also suggested that you choose books with pictures that are big enough to be seen from the back of the group and choose stories that have lots of joining in – farmyard animal noises, counting or actions.

Running sessions – health and safety issues

Health and safety procedures should already be in place as part of the management operation in any library building, and practitioners should be aware of the requirements. A library space that is regularly used for early years sessions should already have a risk assessment checklist in place. Before holding any kind of session for under-fives it is good practice to do a 'baby and toddler audit', and a practical way to undertake this risk assessment is to get down to the child's level and look at the space you will be using for your library sessions. Check for potential hazards, such as plug sockets that may be particularly appealing to little fingers, shelving that may be used for climbing on and heating sources such as radiators. Ensure you have child-size chairs and a clean mat or carpeting for story time. It is important to provide a safe environment for young children and their families, and health and safety requirements should be reviewed and documented regularly.

Planning layout and seating for parent and toddler sessions

Mums, dads and carers should be encouraged to stay with their young children for the story time and activity sessions, so it is important to plan the seating arrangements for the adults before the session starts (as illustrated in Figure 6.1). Considering this practical aspect of planning can make a difference to the success of the session. Remember that not all grown-ups may be able to sit on the floor with their young children or grandchildren on their laps, so do provide some adult-size chairs if they are available. Seating for adults is best kept to the sides of your storytelling area or arranged in a semi-circle to facilitate interaction. A closed circle will help to contain those babies who are starting to crawl! Experience has shown that seating adults at the back of the room sends the message that they are observers rather than participants, and will encourage them to talk among themselves rather than joining in your session.

The young children can be settled on a storytelling mat or special area of carpet. As they are at floor level it helps if you are seated above them – this means it is easier for you to see them and they will be able to see the storybook and any other props you are using. Some venues have a designated storytelling chair. Ensure that you have given yourself enough room to work in and to enable you to easily reach the resources you will use during the session. It is worth checking other practical aspects of the activity venue; for example, it is better for any sunlight to be shining on you

Figure 6.1 Storytelling strategies – planning seating arrangements

and not into the children's eyes, so think about the layout of the space. Experienced practitioners also recommend trying to avoid the inevitable distractions of shared library spaces by seating children with their backs to windows and busy counter areas. It is also a good idea to give parents and carers permission to take their child out of the activity if the child is unhappy, so consider preparing another area with books and toys for young children who aren't ready to sit and listen with the group.

Timing – how long do your sessions last?

Young children have short attention spans and you may be running sessions for groups with a range of ages; the four-month-old baby may be joining her three-year-old brother for rhyme time. Practitioners discussing this question at an Early Years Library Network training day suggested that most sessions should last between 30 minutes and 1 hour. It is a good idea to vary the content of your events as this helps to maintain the children's attention. Don't just fill hour-long sessions with stories, but include songs, rhymes and craft activities. Carol Wootton's advice for making a quality story time is:

> Think about the ages of the children you will be reading to and have stories appropriate to all ages. Be aware how long each story will take to read. A half-hour session is long enough for young children and can be divided up into about 20 minutes of storytelling and 10 minutes for the activity, as a rough guide. But go with the flow, no two sessions are the same in early years work - if you have a lively group that have just found their feet, it's not easy to keep their concentration, however good you are!

Involving parents and carers in your sessions

Some library practitioners suggest that you set out ground rules at the start of each session. Families attending for the first time may appreciate some idea of what to expect and what is acceptable behaviour. One practical tip is to check that all mobile phones have been turned off, as a courtesy, at the start of the activity time. Let the adults and carers know that you can build in time for them to talk together at the beginning or end of the session; this social interaction is very important for building relationships between the families and with the early years librarians. There is evidence to show the value of such contacts in supporting families where referral services are involved; we discussed partnerships with parents in Chapter 2.

During the library visit parents can be actively encouraged to let their babies and young children enjoy the experience of touching and handling the books. Carol Wootton's advice is:

> Do not turn young babies away, the younger you get them the better - it's lovely to see them develop over the weeks taking more notice and getting the parents to let them handle the books.

From a practical viewpoint, it is a good idea to suggest that parents sit with their children while you are doing stories and rhymes; this will encourage a sharing environment and should, hopefully, help to deal with any potentially disruptive behaviour.

Activities with glitter and glue

In addition to story time and rhyme time sessions, craft activities are a fun way to encourage families into your library setting. The early years librarians in Wakefield provide the following advice based on their 'Sticky Fingers' book-related craft sessions: craft activities are best undertaken with adult supervision and so this is a great opportunity to involve parents and carers. Safety is important, so give glue and scissors to the adults. Attention spans will be limited, but simple book-related craft activities can help children learn to follow easy instructions and develop hand–eye co-ordination and motor skills. Using crayons and pencils gives small children the chance to practise holding writing tools. This type of session also helps to develop colour recognition and counting skills. It is a good idea to choose a craft activity that the children can do themselves. Have a picture or a finished example to show them what they can do. Young children will lose interest if an adult has to do most of the work, so encourage parents not to take over.

Making books

A great way of helping children to understand how books work is to make them during an activity session. Many educators incorporate the making of books with children of all ages into their teaching of reading programmes. Whitehead (2007) explains that many young children discover for themselves how to make a book by folding one or two sheets in half and writing and drawing on the pages. During an activity session you can provide different kinds of coloured paper and let the children choose their pictures and the layout of pages. They can discover the power of becoming authors! Another idea is to make photograph books, as young children like to look at pictures of themselves.

Until they grasp the idea of turning pages without tearing the paper, young children will need board or other indestructible books. Goldschmied and Jackson (2004) suggest an easy way of making indestructible picture books by using plastic envelopes. Use family photographs or pictures cut from magazines or catalogues and stuck onto card. Two sheets, back to back, go in each plastic envelope and the pictures can be changed or grouped in categories for older children. This is a good fun activity in a family craft session.

Making a reading tree in your library

When meeting young children and their families on a regular basis, making a reading tree in your library can be a good activity to encourage interaction and involvement. This is easy to start, as all you need to do is to draw a tree trunk and branches on a piece of paper or card and tape it to the wall. You can then involve the children in cutting out different leaf shapes from green card. Keep these leaves in an easy-to-reach place. Each time you read a story book in a session, write the book title and author's name on a paper leaf and add it to the tree. For every book they read together, encourage families to also add their story leaves to the reading tree. Begin by adding the leaves near the bottom and work towards the top. It will be great fun to see the reading tree growing week by week and it is a very visual reminder of the power of stories. This activity can also be done at home, as families can grow their own reading trees.

Dealing with other library users

One issue involved in developing library services for the under-fives may be complaints. Other library users may be concerned that the library has become a crèche and may object to the messy play and craft activities which are an integral part of your early years sessions. It is important that you plan to respond promptly to any such criticism, following your local authority guidelines for dealing with complaints. One solution might be to provide a trolley of books and materials available for other users when you are holding your sessions. It is a good idea to let other library users know when your sessions are held, so put up notices and provide leaflets; they can then make an informed choice not to use the library at these times. You can give examples of other library sessions that are more suited to older people, such as book clubs and coffee mornings.

Planning and evaluation

There is an increasing demand for evidence of effectiveness in provision, and in other chapters of this book we have commented on the importance of meeting the needs of the user community and evaluating what is being provided. This is done to assess how well you are meeting the objectives and targets set for your service. In library services provided for young children and their families, parent satisfaction is one of the key indicators that the library is meeting its objectives. The Appendix (page 167) shows how one library authority has planned an early years programme to include monitoring and evaluation.

Powell (2006), in providing an overview of evaluation research, says that it should enhance knowledge and decision making and lead to practical application. Libraries have traditionally gathered and maintained statistical records and the early years setting will be interested in having data on the number of registered borrowers, the number of books loaned, the number of visitors, events and family learning activities and the numbers attending. Monitoring can enable you to provide evidence about the level of activities – the amount of things you are doing. In order to justify expenditure in the early years library you do need to provide quantitative evidence – measuring how many sessions were offered, how many participants from the target group used particular services, how much of the budget was allocated to stock acquisition for early years resources, and so on. So at one level your organization will need information about how you have used the resources allocated. Data about your services and projects can be collated and analysed to provide information for annual reports and feedback to funding partners. However, Feinberg and Feldman provide something of a challenge when they say:

> Librarians think of evaluation as coming at the end of the process so it is easy to put off and neglect. But the planning process is cyclical. Evaluation stream-lines all activities of the library, completes the planning process for any one activity, and provides the tools for change and growth in public library services. . . .Without the identification of goals and objectives at the beginning of the process, there can be no meaningful evaluation at the end.
>
> (1996, 103)

We feel that there is also a need to go beyond simply measuring the various library processes through performance indicators. There is much interest now in the social impact of library activities. One way of exploring the big question of how libraries contribute to the cohesion and development of their communities is to use the concept of social capital. Measuring impact is much more difficult than collating statistics – how do you know that you are making a difference? How can you prove that you are making a difference? When planning monitoring and evaluation approaches, consider how you will demonstrate the impact of your work and how the qualitative evidence and quantitative data can be interpreted to tell to story of your library provision.

We can look again at some of the evidence gathered by Wakefield Library and Information Services. The early years librarians there have made a significant impact on the lives of many young children and their parents, in areas where literacy levels are particularly low. Here are some points from their impact assessment:

- Approximately 95% of families using our early years libraries in Wakefield have never used libraries before and their perceptions of books, reading and learning are being positively changed.
- Many families are without access to computers in the home. Parents (and children) have been able to develop IT skills in a non-threatening library environment, either to access information or to get help with preparing CVs and job applications
- Professional help has enabled local parents to enrol on IT/Basic Skills training courses, and to take a leading role in the community through fund-raising, chairing meetings, volunteering within the Sure Start community and successfully gaining employment.
- Children with little or no confidence and poor communication skills have started to interact at story sessions and developed new social skills in the friendly environment.
- Families who feel isolated, including Asian families, asylum seekers and Travellers, have discovered a safe, non-threatening environment in which to access support with literacy and information.
- Where families have needed additional support from other agencies, librarians have been able to assist with the referral process.

We have endeavoured to sprinkle examples of impact evidence throughout the chapters of this book by providing comments and feedback from practitioners and parents and carers. We hope that, as effective practitioners, you will be proactive in using guidance on how to gather such evidence in support of your early years library services. Their Reading Futures provides a web-based evidence collection toolkit, and recognizes that most of the evidence needed will be about the impact of services on people. The toolkit provides information on tools and processes to use in generating evidence. The more refined your evidence collection, the clearer the picture you will have of the impact your service is making. Markless and Streatfield (2006) also write about evaluating the impact of your library, discussing success criteria, impact factors and what counts as impact evidence. They provide practical guidance on thinking about evidence and on deciding your approach to gathering it using techniques such as questioning, interviewing and observation.

It is also a good idea to evaluate your professional practice at the operational level. You may be working as part of a team or have responsibility for leading a team in delivering particular services. Systematic evaluation will improve services for children. Teamwork needs to be reviewed regularly so that you can learn from success and improve on weaknesses. You can seek feedback by carrying out regular evaluations of your sessions. The Early Years Library Network suggests that at the very least you should keep a log of the stories and rhymes used in sessions, note how many attended and record any local circumstances that may have affected the turnout. It's also a good idea to keep a log of the weather, as bright sunshine may encourage your regulars to head to the local park, whereas pouring rain may keep people at home. If you have a team of staff you can review the sessions that colleagues are delivering and give feedback on them. One suggestion is to videotape sessions so as to enable your team to analyse the content and reflect on the outcomes and impact. It is important to act on the results. Some questions to ask in reviewing and evaluating teamwork in delivering the early years library sessions might be:

* What went well?
* What didn't go so well and could be improved?
* How could we do this differently next time?

- Who else needs to know about this activity – sharing the messages with your partner organizations and user community.

Personal development planning – managing your own CPD

This final section is about planning your own personal development. Continuing professional development is about ensuring your own personal development and continued competence. One aspect of your development as an early years library practitioner is to network. According to the Chartered Institute of Library and Information Professionals (CILIP), networking is a means of meeting other people to open up opportunities and to obtain or exchange ideas or information. A professional network can help you to build a strong support structure that will enhance your career in the years to come. The most successful information professionals will use networks to:

- get expert advice
- exchange ideas
- get a second opinion
- test new ideas
- gain moral support
- engage in collaborative problem solving.

It is not always possible for early years librarians to attend professional events, but conferences, seminars and training events are a good place to network and can help to broaden your contacts. Look closely at your development needs and those of your colleagues and find out who supplies the required training; this might be the CILIP Youth Libraries Group, the National Literacy Trust, The Reading Agency or other organizations promoting early years literacy. Running joint training sessions with colleagues from other professions can be a good way to network and get productive partnerships off the ground. Consider planning a series of short meetings to exchange ideas or to make a five-minute presentation on your work area. Take a proactive approach and make use of online resources such as Their Reading Futures (TRF), found at **www.theirreadingfutures.org.uk**. The TRF

Best Practice centre aims to support and enable the library community to deliver the very best services to children and young people. It provides access to resources, ideas and case studies that you can use to develop your advocacy role and working practice.

The reflective practitioner

In many professions reflection is approached consciously and deliberately. 'Reflective practice', as it is termed, is regarded as an important dimension of professionalism and a key to learning (Drew and Bingham, 2001). Reflection involves questioning, and thoughtful criticism and analysis. It enhances learning and is an essential part of CPD. Reflection can be described as a thinking and learning process, following an activity, that enables you to use your past to inform and develop your future. It is at the heart of learning from experience because it is the way that you draw out the maximum information from experience. The insight that we gain from this 'reflective questioning' can help us to make decisions, resolve problems or plan our work more effectively. Reflection can also help you to develop self-awareness and have greater clarity about what you want to achieve. Margaret Watson, a former President of CILIP says that:

> since information is at the core of the information society, information workers and other knowledge workers will be key players in this society. In order for information professionals to play their role effectively, they will have to be individually and collectively pro-active in addressing the competency issues that enable them to remain relevant in a dynamic environment . . .

Moyo (2002) says that reflective practice can help us to:

- determine why we do things in professional practice
- make informed, reasoned decisions in practice when there are competing alternatives
- better understand and ultimately improve our practice.

By developing skills of critical analysis the reflective practitioner can examine a situation, identify existing knowledge, challenge assumptions, and envision and explore options. You can help to prompt reflection by keeping a learning diary, asking questions, seeking feedback and allowing yourself time to consider situations. Reflective journal writing can enhance reflection and critical thinking and self-awareness. Becoming a reflective practitioner should help you to become a more effective manager.

So, to summarize this chapter, you have to deliver the objectives of the organization, and to do that successfully you have to plan all the types of resources - policy, people and places - that we have discussed throughout the book. Of course, planning is vital and it is best accomplished through collaboration and communication with others. Policy needs to be implemented - and effective planning arms you with courage and confidence and helps you to be in control.

Issues and questions

- How will you evaluate the success of your service, particularly when working in partnership with other agencies?
- How will you keep effective and manageable records of what works well in your activity sessions?
- How can you gather evidence of the social impact of your services and the added value you are providing? This may be vital for your service's future sustainability.

Key points to remember

- Make sure that your objectives are SMART.
- Use the guidance available from other practitioners - remember to access them through the organizational sources cited in this chapter and throughout the book - you don't have to reinvent the wheel!
- Take responsibility for your own professional development. Nothing stands still and change is inevitable - so be proactive in deciding how you meet change, but sustain what you value.
- Don't avoid (or be frightened of) handling your own budget, or someone else will do it for you and you may not get what you want!

Final comments

Remember the importance of listening to your client groups. Listen to people – community members, parents and children. Even very young children, as you will have seen from some of the case studies and scenarios presented throughout the book, are very capable of indicating to you what they are interested in and whether or not you are meeting their needs.

We hope that this book has given you confidence to do the job of an early years librarian, make a difference and face the future. Early years practitioners – educators, carers and librarians really do have very important roles to play.

Appendix

Early Years Library Services fit with central provision

Objective	Activity	Central Provision	Every Child Matters	
Supporting parents and carers in helping children and young people to enjoy and achieve	Trained and knowledgeable staff provide guidance and help Parent/carer collections provide information on childcare etc. Bookstart gifting promotes and supports parents and carers in introducing stories and books to children at the earliest age and encourages sharing and bonding. Parents and children have been very much involved in the planning and design of our EY Libraries. Ongoing consultation takes place and feedback used in the development of the service Outreach work and provision of satellite collections in the community reduce barriers for those who may find it difficult to access formalized services	Family Support and outreach	Enjoy and Achieve	
Preparing children for school and helping them to meet early learning goals	Provision of a wide range of books and ICT in all of our Early Years Libraries and Children's Centre Story Corners Story times and story-related activities in EY Libraries and children's centres Bookstart treasure boxes Count Me In numeracy packs Incentives for borrowing story books - Baby Book Crawl initiative Nursery class visits Contribution to the Families Enjoying Everything Together (FEET) Programme	Early Education	Enjoy and Achieve	

Output	Outcomes (How will we know that this work has made a difference/been achieved? What will have changed for parents or children using the activity or service?)	Monitoring and evaluation (How will we demonstrate the impact of our work? What qualitative and quantitative outcomes will we set?)
Number of Bookstart packs gifted to babies, 2 year olds and 3 year olds	Parent/carers' increased understanding of the importance of early literacy for children	Improved Foundation Stage results
	Parent and carers feel supported through access to information	Show evidence of how suggestions from feedback from families and stakeholders has been put into practice
Use of parent/carer collections	A more positive relationship developed between parent and child	Gather evidence from users of the impact the use of the library has made in their lives, development of language/numeracy skills/IT skills, general confidence etc.
Number of families completing surveys and feedback forms etc.	Parents feel sense of ownership of the library	
Number of families accessed via outreach work	Parents and carers feel able to access more formalized services	
Number of active users	Improved early experiences for children	Quality outcomes will be measured using the Inspiring Learning for All toolkit – Generic Learning Outcomes include:
Number of books, and other materials loaned	Children will demonstrate enjoyment in listening to stories and looking at books	• Knowledge and understanding • Attitudes and values • Skills • Enjoyment and Inspiration
Number of children participating in activities	Establishing a love of books and stories from the earliest age and making a significant impact on young children's early learning and development, encouraging and improving reading, listening, speaking and language skills	Feedback from users and stakeholders
Number of treasure boxes gifted and packs loaned		Improvement in Foundation Stage results
		Reports from Foundation Stage teachers
Number of children involved in the initiative	Children understand numeracy concepts and enjoy counting-related activities	
Number of nursery class visits	Young children develop the habit of visiting a library and enjoy the experience	

(Continued on next page)

Objective	Activity	Central Provision	Every Child Matters	
Steps are taken to provide children and young people with a safe environment	Each library has been designed for baby-friendliness, to dismiss stereotypical image and make a fun place to visit Parents who feel isolated, are particularly encouraged to visit and enjoy the non-threatening environment Our EY Libraries act as a valuable community meeting space for e.g. local childminders - weekly network meeting	Family Support	Stay Safe	
Parents, carers and families are supported to be economically active	Providing support for access to information and informal learning for those parents and carers who might lack confidence and self-esteem and encouraging them to address their own educational and information needs • Careers information • Help with CVs and job applications • Support to develop IT skills Family Learning Programmes Providing volunteering opportunities	Help with access to training and employment	Economic Well Being	
Parents are helped to ensure their children are healthy	Parent and carer information collections to support child development, dealing with difficult situations e.g. bereavement etc. Access to information about diet, the effects of smoking, exercise and other health issues Health-related activities	Child and Family Health Services	Being Healthy	

Output	Outcomes (How will we know that this work has made a difference/been achieved? What will have changed for parents or children using the activity or service?)	Monitoring and evaluation (How will we demonstrate the impact of our work? What qualitative and quantitative outcomes will we set?)
Number of families visiting the library	Recognized locally and nationally as safe welcoming places within the community where young people are respected and treated as individuals. (Used as example of best practice for Family Friendly service and environment.)	Feedback from surveys and ongoing consultation etc. and making changes if required
Use of the library by community groups	Use of the library by more vulnerable families Increased opportunity for children to socialize	
Numbers accessing the library	Prents and carers gain confidence and start to achieve	Feedback and ongoing consultation with users and stakeholders as above
Use of career information Use of ICT Number of IT surfer sessions	Parents and carers take up training opportunities, or enter the workplace Parent and carers take up learning opportunities	Use of Inspiring Learning For All toolkit
Number of Family Learning programmes and numbers attending Number of volunteers	Parents and carers take up volunteer opportunities	
Use of health-related materials	Parents and carers take an interest in the health of their families and take positive actions to lead a healthier lifestyle	Feedback and ongoing consultation with users and stakeholders as above
Numbers attending health related activities		

References

Aiming High for Children (2007) *Aiming High for Children: supporting families*, HM Treasury/Department for Education and Skills.

Allan, B. (2004) *Project Management Tools and Techniques for Today's ILS Professional*, Facet Publishing.

Allan, B. (2007) *Supervising and Leading Teams in ILS*, Facet Publishing.

Bishop, M. and Rimes, M. (2006) *Better Building Design for Young Children*, Community Playthings.

Booktrust (2007) *Looking at Books: The Big Picture Guide to exploring picture books*, http://booktrustadmin.kentlyons.com/downloads/looking%20at%20books.pdf.

Brock, A. and Power, M. (2007) In Conteh, J. (ed.), *Promoting Learning for Bilingual Pupils 3–11: opening doors to success*, PCP/Sage Publications.

Brock, A. and Rankin, C. (2008) *Communication, Language and Literacy from Birth to Five*, Sage Publications.

Bunnett, R. and Kroll, D. (2006) *Transforming Spaces: rethinking the possibilities*, Community Playthings.

CABE (Commission for Architecture and the Built Environment) (2003) *Creating Excellent Buildings: a guide for clients*, CABE.

CILIP (Chartered Institute of Library and Information Professionals) (2002) *Start with the Child. Report on the CILIP Working Group on Library Provision for Children and Young People*, CILIP.

Clay, M. M. (1991) *Becoming Literate: the construction of inner control,* Heinemann.

Community Playthings (2006) *Spaces: room layout for early childhood education. Your guide to space planning and room layout,* Community Playthings.

Conteh, J. (ed.) (2006) *Promoting Learning for Bilingual Pupils 3–11: opening doors to success,* PCP/Sage Publications.

Conteh, J. and Brock, A. (eds) (2006) Introduction: principles and practices for teaching bilingual learners. In Conteh, J. (ed.), *Promoting Learning for Bilingual Pupils 3–11: opening doors to success,* PCP/Sage Publications, 1–12.

Cooling, W. (2007) *Books for Babies* (Rosemary Clarke, Head of Bookstart, and Wendy Cooling, Founder and Senior Consultant, talk to Madelyn Travis about the scheme's origins and development), item on Booktrust website at www.booktrusted.co.uk/articles/documents.php4?articleid=48 [accessed 9 October 2007].

Cooper, H. (2004) *Exploring Time and Place through Play: Foundation stage – Key Stage 1,* David Fulton.

Corrall, S. (2000) *Strategic Management of Information Services: a planning handbook,* ASLIB/IMI.

Creaser, C. and Maynard, S. (2006) *A Survey of Library Services to Schools and Children in the UK 2005–06,* Library and Information Statistics Unit (LISU).

DfCSF (Department for Children, Schools and Families) (2007) *The Early Years Foundation Stage: setting the standards for learning, development and care for children from birth to five,* DfCSF Publications.

DCMS (Department for Culture, Media and Sport) (2008) *Public Library Service Standards,* 3rd rev. edn, DCMS.

Department of National Heritage (1995) *Investing in Children: the future of public library services for children and young people,* HMSO.

Dewe, M. (1995) *Planning and Designing Libraries for Children and Young People,* Library Association Publishing.

Dewe, M. (2006) *Planning Public Library Buildings: concepts and issues for the librarian,* Ashgate.

DfEE (Department for Education and Employment) (1999) *SureStart: a guide for trailblazers*, HMSO and www.Surestart.com.

DfES (Department for Education and Skills) (2000) *Single Regeneration Budget*, www.standards.dfes.gov.uk.

DfES (2007) *Early Years Foundation Stage*, DfES Publications.

Drew, S. and Bingham, R. (2001) *The Student Skills Guide*, Gower.

Dudek, M. (2000) *Kindergarten Architecture: space for the imagination*, 2nd edn, Spon Press.

Dudek, M. (2001) *Building for Young Children: a practical guide to planning, designing and building the perfect space,* National Early Years Network.

Feather, J. and Sturgess, P. (1997) *International Encyclopaedia of Information and Library Science*, Routledge.

Feinberg, S., Deerr, K., Jordan, B., Byrne, M. and Kropp, L. (2007) *The Family-Centered Library Handbook: rethinking library spaces and services*, Neal-Schuman Publishers.

Feinberg, S. and Feldman, S. (1996) *Serving Families and Children Through Partnerships: a how-to-do-it manual for librarians*, Neal-Schuman Publishers.

Feinberg, S., Kuchner, J. and Feldman, S. (1998) *Learning Environments for Young Children: rethinking library spaces and services*, American Library Association.

Feinberg, S. and Rogoff, C. (1998) Diversity Takes Children to a Family Friendly Place, *American Libraries*, (August), 50–2.

Fox, C. (1993) *At the Very Edge of the Forest. The influence of literature on storytelling by children*, Cassell.

Framework for the Future (2003) *Framework for the Future: libraries, learning and information in the next decade*, Department for Culture, Media and Sport, PP496, www.culture.gov.uk/reference_library/publications/4505.aspx.

Gammage, P. (2006) Early Childhood Education and Care: politics, policies and possibilities, *Early Years: an international journal of research and development*, **26** (3), 235–48.

Goldschmied, E. and Jackson, S. (2004) *People Under Three – young children in day care*, 2nd edn, Routledge.

Goulding, A. (2006) *Public Libraries in the 21st Century: defining services and debating the future*, Ashgate.

Greene, E. (1991) *Books, Babies and Libraries: serving infants, toddlers, their parents and caregivers*, American Library Association.

Harris, K. and Dudley, M. (2005) *Public Libraries and Community Cohesion – developing indicators*, MLA.

IFLA (2003) *Guidelines for Children's Library Services*, IFLA Children and Young Adults Section.

Kahn, T. (2005) *Fathers' Involvement in Early Years Settings: findings from research*, Report prepared for the Department of Education and Skills, Pre-Schooling Learning Alliance.

King, J. (2007) *The Environment in your Nursery. The effect of sound and colour on young children*, Community Playthings, www.communityplaythings.co.uk/c/resources/articles/ environments/mood.htm.

Kirsch, I. (2002) *Reading for Change: performance and engagement across countries*. Results from PISA 2000 (Programme for International Student Assessment – how well young adults are doing at end of compulsory schooling), OECD.

Kropp, L. G. (2004) Family Place Libraries: building strong families, strong libraries, *JLAMS Journal of the Library Administration and Management Section of the New York Library Association*, **1** (1), 39–47.

Lane, J. (2008) *Young Children and Racial Justice. Taking action for racial equality in the early years – understanding the past, thinking about the present, planning for the future*, National Children's Bureau.

Lewis, A. and Lindsay, G. (2000) *Researching Children's Perspectives*, Open University Press.

Lushington, N. (2002) *Libraries Designed for Users: a 21st century guide*, Neal-Schuman.

Lushington, N. (2008) *Libraries Designed for Kids*, Facet Publishing/Neal Schuman.

McElwee, G. (2004) It's Never Too Early, *Library and Information Update*, **3** (11), 23–5.

McKearney, M. (2007) The Reading Agency is Five, *Library and Information Update*, **6** (12), 38–41.

Markless, S. and Streatfield, D. (2006) *Evaluating the Impact of Your Library*, Facet Publishing.

MLA South East (2007) *In Brief – Public Library Service Impact Measures* (a briefing sheet which should be read in conjunction with further information from the MLA website), www.mlasoutheast.org.uk/assets/documents/10000A8.

MORI (2003) *Physical Capital: Liveability in 2005*, MORI.

Moyo, L. (2002) CPE Anywhere, Anytime: online resources for the Information Society. In *Continuing Professional Education for the Information Society: 5th World Conference on CPE for the LIS Profession*, IFLA, 224–31.

Music Manifesto (2006) *Making Every Child's Music Matter. Music Manifesto report no 2. A consultation for action*, Music Manifesto.

National Association of Toy and Leisure Libraries (2007) *Toy Libraries – their benefits for children and communities*, NATLL and Capacity, www.natll.org.uk/pdfs/CapacityReportJune07.pdf.

NLT (National Literacy Trust) (2002) *Getting a Head Start. A good ideas guide for promoting reading to young families*, NLT.

NLT (National Literacy Trust) (2006) *Research Shows Social Benefits of Reading: National Literacy Trust Viewpoint – October 2006*, www.literacytrust.org.uk/About/NLTperspectives06.html.

NLT (2007a) *Getting Blokes on Board: involving fathers and male carers with their children*, National Literacy Trust, www.nationalliteracytrust.org.uk/familyreading/Blokes.html.

NLT (National Literacy Trust) (2007b) *Policy proposal to develop the Family Reading Campaign into a national strategy to support family literacy*, www.literacytrust.org.uk/familyreading/FamilyLiteracyPolicyPaper.pdf.

Nicholas, D. (2000) *Assessing Information Needs: tools, techniques and concepts for the internet age*, Aslib.

North, S. and Allen, N. (2005) A Better Beginning with Books and Libraries for Western Australian Babies, *Australasian Public Libraries and Information Services APLIS 2005*, **18** (4),131–6.

Olds, A. (2001) *Child Care Design Guide*, McGraw-Hill.

Potter, C. (2008) Getting Young Children Talking in Early Years Settings. In Brock, C. and Rankin, A. (eds), *Communication, Language and Literacy from Birth to Five*, Sage Publications.

Powell, R. R. (2006) Evaluation Research: an overview, *Library Trends*, **55** (1), 102–20.

Rankin, C., Brock, A., Halpin, E. and Wootton, C. (2007) *The Role of the Early Years Librarian in Developing an Information Community: a case study of effective partnerships and early years literacy within a Sure Start project in Wakefield*, paper presented in the conference proceedings of the Canadian Association of Information Sciences, Montreal, 2007.

Riches, R. (2007) *Early Years Outreach Practice – supporting early years practice working with Gypsy, Roma and Traveller families. With transferable ideas for other outreach early years workers*, Save the Children Fund.

Roberts, S. A. (1998) *Financial Cost Management for Libraries and Information Services*, 2nd edn, Bowker-Saur.

Robinson, A. (n.d.) *Picture This* project – unpublished report, Blackburn with Darwen Borough.

Rohl, M. and Barratt-Hugh, C. (2006) Evaluating Better Beginnings. In Abbott, L. and Langston, A. (eds), *Parents Matter: supporting the birth to three matters framework*, Open University.

Ross, C. S., McKechnie, L. E. F. and Rothbauer, P. M. (2006) *Reading Matters: what research reveals about reading, libraries and community*, Libraries Unlimited.

Sawyer, V., Pickstone, C. and Hall, D. (2007) *Promoting Speech and Language: a themed study in fifteen Sure Start local programmes*, www.surestart.gov.uk/_doc/p0002441.pdf.

Sherriff, N. (2007) *Supporting Young Fathers: examples of promising practice*, Trust for the Study of Adolescence.

Shonkoff, J. P. and Phillips, D. A. (2000) *From Neurons to Neighbourhoods: the science of early childhood development*, National Academy Press.

Spacey, R. (2005) *Family Learning and Public Libraries: a scoping paper*, National Institute of Adult Continuing Education (NIACE).

Stevens, A. (2003) Libraries Put Vision into Action, *Literacy Today*, **37**, (December), www.literacytrust.org.uk/Pubs/stevens.html.

Sullivan, H. and Skelcher, C. (2002) *Working Across Boundaries: collaboration in public services*, Palgrave Macmillan.

Sure Start (2007) *Toolkit for Reaching Priority and Excluded Families, Version 2* (January), Together for Children (national partnership of childcare services), www.tda.gov.uk/upload/resources/pdf/t/tfc_toolkit.pdf.

Swiniarski, L. (2006) Helping Young Children Become Citizens of the World, *Scholastic Early Childhood Today*, (November/December), 36-8.

Sylva, K. (1994) The Impact of Early Learning on Children's Later Development. In Ball, C. (ed.), *Start Right: the importance of early learning*, Royal Society of Arts, 84-96.

Sylva, K., Melhuish, E. C., Sammons, P., Siraj-Blatchford, I. and Taggert, B. (2004) *The Effective Provision of Pre-school Education [EPPE] Project: final report*, DfES/Institute of Education, University of London.

Taggert, B. (2004) Editorial: early years education and care: three agendas, *British Educational Research Association Journal*, **30** (5), 619-22.

Van Orden, P. J. and Bishop, K. (2001) *The Collection Program in Schools: concepts, practices and information sources*, 3rd edn, Libraries Unlimited.

Wade, B. and Moore, M. (1998) *A Gift for Life: Bookstart, the first five years - a description and evaluation of an exploratory British project to encourage sharing books with babies*, Book Trust.

White, D. R. (2002) Working Together to Build a Better World: the importance of youth services in the development and education of children and their parents, *OLA Quarterly*, **8** (3) (Fall), 15-19.

Whitehead, M. (2007) *Developing Language and Literacy for Young Children*, 3rd edn, Paul Chapman.

Wilkie, S. (ed.) (2002) *Take Them to the Library*, Youth Libraries Group.

Williams, F. and Churchill, H. (2006) *Empowering Parents in Sure Start Local Programmes*, National Evaluation of Sure Start (NESS) Institute for the Study of Children, Families and Social Issues, Birkbeck, University of London. Research Report NESS/2006/FR/018.

Index